Praise for Kerry Cohen

Girl Trouble

A clear and concise survey of one woman's journey through a life's worth of difficult and sometimes devastating female friendships. Cohen bravely details how one's family of origin impacts on our later relationships, and accurately demonstrates how we must first sort ourselves out before we can establish healthy bonds with others.

> BLAKE NELSON, author of *The City Wants You Alone*

This book is so goddamn good, you'll plotz.

> LIDIA YUKNAVITCH, author of *The Chronology of Water*

Kerry Cohen traces a delicate thread that runs thorough so many women's lives…. Cohen's concise portraits bring to life all those girls we knew—and loved madly and hated, and envied and feared—carrying the reader from the years when girlhood itself felt as tender and raw as a bruise, through the emotional minefield of friendships in early womanhood, to the later laughter and ease that we finally are able to share with our female friends. A small treasure.

> MARYA HORNBACHER, author of *Madness: A Bipolar Life*

I was mesmerized by *Girl Trouble*. Kerry Cohen writes about friendship and longing with such searching intensity, I simply could not put the book down until I'd read it all. *Girl Trouble* is raw, real, and revelatory.

> CHERYL STRAYED, author of *Wild*

Loose Girl

Cohen's brutal honesty about her relentless request for companionship is refreshingly relatable.

> ENTERTAINMENT WEEKLY

Cohen recounts her harrowing litany of hookups through clear, poignant, spare-no-details prose.

MARIE CLAIRE

Sensual yet sophisticated ... explores why people yearn to be loved.

SELF

A quick and riveting read.... Thanks Kerry Cohen, for being real.

PLAYGIRL

A fascinating cautionary tale ... *Loose Girl* will make you contemplate your own relationships.

ZINK

Her candor may help under-21 readers steer clear of the whole mess, while those who survived similar ordeals will appreciate her tale of survival.

BOOKLIST

An illuminating memoir of her misspent younger years when a desperate search for love led to a series of promiscuous sexual relationships with men.

THE SEATTLE POST-INTELLIGENCER

Compelling.... Cohen is a fine writer. She is introspective, and there's a wry humor that penetrates *Loose Girl*.

THE OREGONIAN

Cohen's training as a psychotherapist is clearly evident. She reveals an impressive analytic prowess as she exposes the damaging self-effacement that underlies the seeming assertion involved in attracting men to her and then driving them away.... An important look at the dynamics of female sexual power and promiscuity in general.

KIRKUS REVIEWS

Cohen's memoir is a deeply poignant, desperately sad account ... commendably honest and frequently excruciating to read.

PUBLISHERS WEEKLY

Seeing Ezra

Oregon Book Award Finalist for Creative Nonfiction

Seeing Ezra is the story of motherhood beyond all reserves. Bravo to Cohen for giving us such a deep, rich tale of motherhood.

>   VICKI FORMAN, author of *This Lovely Life*

This is a book to think with, a brave meditation on love and acceptance. Not just for mothers – this is a beautiful story about being human.

>   ARIEL GORE, author of *Bluebird: Women and the New Psychology of Happiness*

Seeing Ezra is an important book.

>   JENNIFER LAUCK, author of *Blackbird*

I am not a mother and have never raised a special-needs child, yet Cohen's frank memoir kept me riveted.

>   BRENDA MILLER, author of *Blessing of the Animals*

Ultimately, *Seeing Ezra* is a love story and a portrait of Ezra as Ezra, with all the simplicity and complexity that entails. It is a story skillfully told by a mother who understands her son for who he is and for what he brings to the world on his own terms.

>   ROBERT RUMMEL-HUDSON, author of *Schuyler's Monster: A Father's Journey with His Wordless Daughter*

Dirty Little Secrets: Breaking the Silence on Teenage Girls and Promiscuity

Ms. Cohen's *Dirty Little Secrets* is a perfect catalyst for mother/daughter discussions. It is a safe place to start a scary talk … a wake-up call…. Settle in, relax, and embrace its shocking content.

>   THE NEW YORK JOURNAL OF BOOKS

Very few people can write about teen girls' sexual promiscuity with the candor, empathy, and intelligence Kerry Cohen does.

>   ROSALIND WISEMAN, author of *Queen Bees and Wannabes*

As compassionate as it is enlightening, Kerry Cohen's *Dirty Little Secrets* argues for female safety and desire, and provides a road map for authentically healthy, vital sexuality.

>   JENNIFER BAUMGARDNER, author of *Look Both Ways*

The Truth of Memoir:
How to Write About Yourself and Others with
Honesty, Emotion, and Integrity

This book bravely enters the sometimes dark and tangled world of memoir writing – and finds light and clarity on the other side.

> SUE WILLIAM SILVERMAN, author of *Fearless Confessions: A Writer's Guide to Memoir*

Kerry Cohen's The Truth of Memoir is a smart, soulful, psychologically astute guide to first-person writing.

> SUSAN SHAPIRO, author of *Only As Good as Your Word*

Easy

The writing is realistic, insightful, and nonjudgmental.

> LIBRARY JOURNAL

It's Not You It's Me

Despite offering moments of levity, Cohen gives plenty of weight and attention to Zoe's darker feelings – her broad spectrum of emotions and gradual recovery ring true.

> PUBLISHERS WEEKLY

Girls will relate to the teen's heartbreak and healing.

> SCHOOL LIBRARY JOURNAL

Library of Congress
Cataloging-in-Publication Data

Hawthorne Books
& Literary Arts

Cohen, Kerry, author.
Girl trouble: an illustrated memoir / Kerry Cohen; illustrated by Tyler Cohen.
pages cm
ISBN 9780997068337 (paperback)
1. Girls-Psychology.
2. Women-Psychology.
3. Interpersonal relations-Psychological aspects.
4. Man-woman relationships-Psychological aspects.

I. Title.

HQ777.C596 2016
155.43/3-DC23
2016020819

9
8
7
6
5
4
3
2
1

2201 Northeast 23rd Avenue
3rd Floor
Portland, Oregon 97212
hawthornebooks.com

Form:
Adam McIsaac/Sibley House

Printed in China

Set in Paperback

To all our sisters

Girl Trouble

An illustrated memoir
Kerry Cohen

ILLUSTRATED BY Tyler Cohen

 HAWTHORNE BOOKS & LITERARY ARTS
Portland, Oregon | MMXVI

GIRL TROUBLE

PREFACE

Tyler

IN THE BEGINNING, THERE WAS TYLER AND ME. I FOLLOWED her around, wishing I could do the things she did. I remember chasing her through tall grass. I remember watching her on the jungle gym. She was always more athletic than I was. That was the time she accidentally knocked a board down and it hit me square on the nose because I had bent my head back to see her, see her going up and up away from me. It's my one scar. I wore her hand-me-downs, her clothes mine, her scent mine. Tyler and Kerry. Unknowable apart.

When I was seven and she was nine, we started fighting. Bad fights where she punched, and I pushed and ran. Our mother gave us separate rooms then. She had to. This, I think, is when we began a necessary separation. Tyler, and then Kerry.

Next there were friends and boys and our parents' divorce. It was an ugly divorce, fraught with affairs and devastation and anger. Our mother chose Tyler for her ally. Our father chose me. We visited our father every other weekend and for dinner on Wednesdays, and we sat in opposition to each other, fierce eyes, hungry hearts. When our mother left us with our father to pursue medical school in the Philippines, Tyler got left in a deeper way. She retreated to her room. She got into things I didn't, like punk music and alternative clothes. And I got into boys, whatever it would take to get into boys.

I called her names I can never take back. I told her she was a lesbian, like that was a bad thing. I told her she was a loser, that she had no friends. I don't remember her ever calling me names back.

I hated her because I hated my mother. For never allowing me to have my feelings, for controlling who I was and where I went, even from overseas. I didn't care that she left me. But Tyler seemed ruined to me, and so I hated her for leaving Tyler alone. Hated that I had to care. Hated the ways in which I felt guilt.

Once, I came home from school, and Tyler had locked herself in our father's bathroom. I knew there were pills in there. I'd already stolen a couple. My father was an addict—pot, cocaine, pills. He was a functional addict, but he was an addict nonetheless. The kind that kept himself removed from us, just enough so that Tyler and I were alone in this wilderness of our adolescent lives. And now Tyler was locked in the bathroom. I knocked once.

"Tyler?" I asked.

I heard a glass clink, then something fell to the floor.

"What?" she said.

"You okay?"

"Fine."

I went back to the living room, my swollen heart in my throat. I waited, bouncing my leg. Waiting, waiting. Finally, I heard the toilet flush and she came out.

"Hey," she said, when she saw me sitting there. The divide between us was so long, so deep. I couldn't imagine how to cross it.

"Hey," I said back.

"I have a headache is all," she said.

I nodded, didn't know what to say.

"Okay," I said finally.

It was the closest we would get for many years.

She left for college. She grew up and out. Eventually, she got married, and then divorced. And then married again. She gave birth to a daughter. I got married, and then divorced. I had two boys, one with autism, and then I married again too.

We did things differently, and she felt criticized by me. I had an autistic child, and I felt that she didn't care.

Also, though, I didn't want to share myself with her. I didn't want closeness or intimacy. Not with her, not with anyone. There was a period of time that was true.

Slowly, we found our way back. We were survivors, after all. Just her and me. Tyler and Kerry. We were the only ones who knew. *Who know.* Something happens as you grow up. Barriers matter less. Differences do too. You reach for people. You know time is limited, and that some things that mattered before stop mattering so much.

Last year I asked Tyler to work on *Girl Trouble* with me. Tyler was my first female friend, after all. My first trouble with a friend. She was there. *She was there.* And now here we are together, matched through blood, chosen through love. Sisters.

Lisa

THERE WAS A TIME WHEN I DIDN'T THINK ABOUT FRIEND-ship. It just happened. Jeffrey in preschool. Chanel in kindergarten. Karen and Erica and Jon and Jonathan and Fosca and Liz. We were just friends, because friendship just *happened*. This was before my parents' messy divorce, before my mother left me, before I had fallen under the sway of boys and their sweet desires. It was before life started its slow trickle around me.

Lisa was my third-grade best friend. We were inseparable. I slept at her house more than she slept at mine. We had practice crushes on one of her older brother's friends. Practiced kissing on her pillows. Lisa could play "You Light Up My Life" on the piano, so she'd play and we'd sing in our falsettos, no care about who might hear.

That Halloween, her oldest brother died in a car crash. His friends, who were twins, and their mother were in the car too. They all died suddenly, inexplicably. Poof. Four lives snuffed out. The rest of us found out when Lisa didn't show up at school the next day, or for two weeks after.

My mother and I went to her house to pay our respects. Their hallway, lined with mirrors, was covered with butcher paper, one of the Jewish traditions done while sitting shiva after a loved one's death. I don't remember what we brought. Probably food. Lisa's mother wept most of the time we were there. Lisa sat near me. I wanted to say the right thing, to say *something*, but everything I could come up with seemed wrong, seemed disrespectful to the fact that she was grieving. In the end, I said nothing. I wonder now if this was why when she returned to school everything was different. Probably she wanted nothing in her life that came before her brother died. Probably she wanted to start over, to forget, to pretend to be someone who only ever had one brother and not two. Probably I'd disappointed her by not saying the things she needed to hear. I didn't know any of this at the time, and of course I still don't know the reason. But I remember sitting at my desk in class, aware of her, my best friend, now gone and replaced by this person I didn't know, who didn't seem to want to know me anymore. And friendships would never be easy again.

Nina

WHEN I THINK OF NINA NOW, I THINK OF HER FINGERS. Long, delicate, cool fingers. She entwined them with mine, soft and fragile, like a baby bird, as we walked down the elementary school hallway. Fingers that lightly held me together against the chaos of my life at home. Which is what best friends were supposed to do.

Days I came home from school unsure what I'd find. My mother crying on the phone. My mother in bed with the door shut tight. When my father came home later the silence between them was so loud I could barely think. I ducked away, not wanting to hear the things said, things like, "You could have called if you were going to be late. I made this fucking dinner." Things like, "How dare you come home night after night like this?" Sometimes my mother screamed at him, so out of control you couldn't understand what she was saying. Sometimes she spat out things I knew I shouldn't have heard, things about another woman and fucking and pain. My father, though, was always quiet. His lips pursed in disgust. He didn't love her anymore, and a part of me was terrified that I didn't either.

But then Nina. Nina with the caramel skin and thin silky hair the same color. She had a high, quiet voice. She wore red tortoiseshell glasses and thin white blouses that buttoned to her neck.

My mother painted the house room by room. Paint chips splayed on the dining room table. She didn't bother with dinner anymore. She stood over the colors, forehead furrowed, and pulled one to the side to examine it. She moved certain ones next to oth-

ers. She left paint chips taped to walls. Everywhere I went in the house, there they were, like emblems of something about to arrive. Tiny passports. She started with the downstairs bathroom. Then she moved on to the guest room. Then the master bedroom. My father came home fewer and fewer nights. When he did come home he slept in the guest room, now a soothing cappuccino brown, while my mother sobbed upstairs. I stayed in my room, afraid to disrupt this strange, bursting silence. Once, though, I came into the hallway to see my mother standing there by the stairs. Her eyes were faraway. She was frozen, a strange statue.

"Mom?" I said carefully. "Are you okay?"

She didn't seem to hear me. I waited. Finally, she walked toward her room and shut the door.

So whenever I could, I stayed at Nina's for dinner. Her mother was a psychiatrist who saw clients in her home office. Her father was rarely home. Sometimes Nina and I hid behind the banister upstairs and watched her mother's patients arrive. I wondered about them, all those people, about what they talked about behind the closed door.

In the summer, Nina planned to go to the camp where she went every year with her old best friend from Saddle River, Anastasia. I'd never met her, but Nina kept a picture of the two of them on her desk in her bedroom. A stack of correspondences, replete with red and pink hearts and sparkly rainbow stickers, sat in the desk's drawer. The day she showed me, I smiled and nodded politely, doing my best to mask my jealousy. I begged my mother to let me go to the camp with Nina.

"You're not the only one around here who wants things right now."

"I know," I said.

But my father paid for me to go; and Nina, Anastasia, and I traveled on the bus into the Adirondacks. They knew the other girls, and I watched as Anastasia leaned to whisper into select girls' ears, her long blond hair falling lightly against her face. The girls listened eagerly, and by the time we stood to exit single file from the bus they were all speaking her name: "Anastasia," they said. "Look." "Anastasia, over here. Come stand by me." But Anastasia leaned against Nina.

We slept twenty girls to a cabin. Rows and rows of bunks, like in an asylum, lined the musty room. Nina and Anastasia had already claimed each other as bunkmates, so I smiled at a small girl with dark eyes and frizzy hair and threw my duffel on the lower bunk.

"Do you know Anastasia?" she asked in a small voice.

I shook my head. "Nina's my best friend," I told her. "And Nina knows her."

"Oh." I saw the confusion in her face as she watched Nina and Anastasia across the room, where Anastasia was French braiding Nina's hair.

During dinner we stood in line to get trays of rice and hot dogs and pale iceberg-lettuce salads with tiny strips of carrot. We sat at the long wooden tables. My hair was in a ponytail and Anastasia leaned close, peering into my face.

"What?" I said.

"What is that?"

"What?" I tried to cover whatever she saw with my hands. I looked at Nina, but she was busy eating, trying to look like she hadn't heard a thing.

"Do you have a hair coming out of your chin?"

"No!" But later, I examined my chin in the cloudy mirror of the bathroom and found an eyebrow hair that had fallen and gotten stuck there. I considered telling Anastasia, to even save the little hair, but I thought better of it.

The next day, we lined up at the swimming pool. I could feel the way my thighs pressed against each other. Anastasia, like Nina, was sleek and lovely, like the horses we could see grazing in a pasture across the way. The other girls admired Nina's braid. They begged Anastasia to do theirs next.

We splashed into the water, one at a time, to reveal our swimming skills so we could join the appropriate instructor. I was given a tag with a yellow sticker to signify I was in the lowest group. The best, like Anastasia, got blue stickers. Intermediate got red. Yellow stayed, while red and blue got to move on to crafts. Their instruction would be later. I watched as Nina and Anastasia walked off together, arm in arm, a gaggle of girls in their wake. Our yellow group got kickboards and traveled up and down the length of the sparkling pool kicking and blowing bubbles.

When we got out an hour later, one of the younger counselors approached me.

"You're burned," she said.

I looked at her, confused.

"Your back," she said. "It's all red."

I pressed my shoulder and watched as the angry pink turned to white, then back to pink.

"Come with me," she said. "I'm taking this one," she called to the other counselors.

I followed her across the way, near where the horses were, into a small shack. She turned me around, clucking and shaking her head.

"I'm a CIT," she told me, which meant she was fourteen years old, a counselor-in-training. She said, "You poor thing." I stood still as she went into a cabinet and then squeezed white cream from a tube. Her fingers were light on my back as she rubbed it in. I squeezed my eyes shut, trying not to cry. "Does it hurt?"

I nodded, afraid to speak. She was so pretty, with feathered black hair and a heart-shaped face. Her eyes were lined with blue and she wore heavy mascara. She smiled at me, and as soon as our eyes met the tears came. She pulled me into a hug and I rested my head against her shoulder.

"It's okay," she said. "Whatever it is, I promise it will be okay."

I closed my eyes.

"Can I stay with you?" I asked.

She searched my face, concerned. "For a little while." She unfolded chairs for us and we sat facing outside toward the horses. She watched them intently.

"Do you ride?" I asked.

Her face lit up. "Yeah. Do you?"

I shrugged. "I've never tried."

"I can teach you."

"I'd love that."

She turned to look at me. "What bunk are you in?"

I told her.

"You guys have lessons Thursdays."

I shook my head, imagining Anastasia here, ruining this, pulling the CIT's attention from me. "I don't want to have lessons with everyone else."

She cocked her head and laughed. "Not sure we can do private lessons."

"I don't want to do anything with them," I said too quickly.

She watched me for a moment. "It gets better," she said. "It does."

When I didn't say anything, she added, "If things get really bad you can come hang out with me."

Later, the CIT walked me back to the bunk. They were all there, Anastasia and Nina, the girl with the frizzy hair. They all looked up when I walked in. I tried to meet Nina's eyes, but she looked away.

In the cafeteria, I didn't bother trying to sit with Nina anymore. Nina was gone, long long gone. She laughed and whispered with Anastasia and their followers. I sat with the CIT who'd been so nice to me, or with the frizzy-haired girl.

One time after lunch I saw Nina outside the dining hall barn vomiting up the red Jell-O we'd had for dessert. She cried, and someone rushed inside to get a counselor. Anastasia came right out, her best friend, there for her. The counselor gestured to everyone to go back inside, to go about their days. I did exactly that. I didn't even look at Nina. I didn't care anymore. I wouldn't. She wasn't mine to care about.

I don't know how long I'd been at the camp. All I know is that it hadn't been that long—maybe a week, maybe two—when

I woke in the morning to the feel of something wet and slimy on my pillow. I blinked, confused, staring at the white mess. After a moment I realized the girls had put shaving cream on my face after I fell asleep. I sat up, furious, humiliated. A few of the girls turned to look and laugh. I felt my face grow hot. I reached for a towel and scrubbed, and I yanked my sheets off the cot.

"What happened?" I heard Anastasia's voice through the laughter. "Did you forget to wash off the shaving cream after shaving your beard?" More laughter.

Tears pressed into my eyes. "Screw you, Anastasia."

"Come on." Her voice was close now. She stood right next to me. "We just had a little fun."

I didn't say anything. I gathered my sheets and the towel and headed for the door.

"You're going to tattle?" Anastasia yelled after me. "Like a little baby?" But I was crying too hard to respond.

"Kerry." Nina's voice, soft and lilting. I turned around and looked at her, the pain heavy in my chest. Her eyes searched mine, but I gave her nothing. "Don't be mad," she said. "It was just a joke."

I walked away, clutching my linens, out into the commons, where a counselor found me and took me to the main office. After a few minutes I calmed down enough to call my mother.

Four hours later she arrived, harried, annoyed, but also concerned. We piled my belongings into the car and took off down the country road. All around us were grassy meadows and forests. The sky was a blinding blue. My mother didn't say anything, just turned up the Fleetwood Mac cassette playing on the stereo. I opened the window and let the warm breeze flutter at my face, thankful for my mother's silence, that she didn't ask about what happened. I knew she'd been dealing with her own catastrophe this summer, with the impending divorce. And now here we both were, ruined, despairing, hurtling in our silence back home.

Years later, when I was eighteen, I visited a lover at Columbia University. He didn't love me. I knew this. But I opened myself to him anyway, eager for attention. Eager to feel his breath on my neck, the flutter of his eyelashes on my cheek. Above his desk was a picture of a woman. I moved to get a closer look. Of course I did. To see who he would love, if not me. In the picture, a woman lay supine on a couch, her eyes soft and sad. With shock I saw that it was Nina, grown up now, still unbearably lovely. I brought my hand to my throat, the jealousy and hatred rising as thick and black and unmovable as it had that summer so many years ago.

Gaby

IT WAS THE LATE SUMMER OF 1982, RIGHT BEFORE I turned twelve, and I had gone with nine other girls and ten boys to a mandatory wilderness program called Dorrs intended to orient us to Horace Mann School, where we would be starting in the fall. We rode on the bus through the heavily forested highways of upstate New York to the camp in Connecticut. Some girls knew one another from elementary school, and they huddled together, giggling and chatting, relieved to have familiar faces nearby. I knew no one. All of these faces were unfamiliar. I didn't know the bus or the place we were headed. At home my parents were in the midst of an ugly divorce, so I didn't know that place either. And then there was puberty, which had been ripping through my body for the past year with all its strange physicality and feelings and desires. I didn't even know who I was anymore.

So when we arrived at the camp and carried our duffels into the cabins, suddenly every move felt sharp and highlighted. Everything mattered: which bed I chose, where I dropped my bag, whether I sat on my bed or started unpacking. The other girls seemed fine. They talked and giggled and did whatever they did without thought. Surely, this was my childish perception, that I was the only one feeling awkward, that I was the only one under a microscope, the only one not right. I wound up with an upper bunk against the wall, close to the door. Then one of the group leaders came in. She clapped her hands.

"Okay, girls. Let's go. Down to the campfire for a meeting."

We applied bug spray and readjusted barrettes and head-bands in the mottled mirrors in the bathroom, and then tromped down the path to the fire pit. The air was heavy with humidity. The boys were already sitting around the pit on the wooden benches, and some of the girls pulled up their tank tops halfway, revealing their bellies. The boys, of course, looked. One girl, Gaby, asked me my name. She had been in the program since nursery school. She pointed out the girls she knew and told me a little about each.

"That one," she said, nodding toward a girl named Tiffany who would become my bully that year, the one who would haunt me for years, "is a bitch. And that one," she referred to the girl next to her, "is a bitch in training. Just stay away from them and you'll be okay." The bitch she referred to had curly dishwater hair. She was one of the ones who had raised her tank top. She sat with the other girl, who I'd later learn was Courtney, hanging on her almost, looking to her constantly. We introduced ourselves, and when I said my name quietly, Tiffany smirked at Courtney. To this day I wonder what it was about me. I had had friends throughout elementary school. In most of my friendships, I'd been fun and happy and unafraid. But that day something shifted. For the first time I saw myself in the world, with others around me. My parents divorcing. My mother's grief. My own sense of newness and change, of the world spinning out of control.

The leaders handed out envelopes and small pads of paper to each of us and explained that we would each write our name on the envelope and hang it from the bulletin board near our bed. Each day of the week we were here we would use the pad to write notes of praise or encouragement to one another, which we would stick inside the person's envelope. We had to write three per day, but we were welcome to write more.

Back in the cabin we all hung our envelopes, and then we left for kitchen duty. We had various chores to complete each day—cleaning the cabin, making meals, and cleaning up after meals. We went out to a clearing in the woods and did blindfolded trust falls, had to get ourselves over a wall using teamwork, and prepared for

a three-day hike. What I remember most, though, are those envelopes. At the end of each day, we checked them. The girls Gaby
had pointed out to me had at least three per day. I tried to think
of things to say to each girl, and some afternoons during our free
time, when most of us wrote our notes, I spent the whole hour and
a half crafting these notes of praise for my bunkmates. We all wrote
things like, *You were really helpful at cleanup today*, or, *You're a nice
girl*. By evening, though, I always had only one, always from Gaby,
and some days I had none at all.

In the last part of the trip, we went on the three-day hike
through the woods. We camped in tents, made our own fires, fished,
and had to use compasses to find our way back to the camp. I have
no memory of any of this. I don't remember the smell of the thick
oaks and maples, the sound of the creek, the shock of cold as I
leaned down to touch the water that rushed by. I don't remember
lying on the cold ground in my sleeping bag or who slept next to me.
I don't remember turning on my flashlight in the night and walking
into the warm night, the bulbous yellow light before me, so I could
pee in the woods. I remember none of it. In truth, I can't be sure it
happened. Twenty-five years later, after I had published my first
memoir and reconnected with various people from my past, Gaby
contacted me. She wrote, "It's so great to see you again! I have such
good memories of you." I didn't know who she was. Her face, her
name, the things she said—none of it called up any sort of familiar-
ity in my mind. She's the one who told me this story, who said she's
sure she had a photograph somewhere (although she never could
find it) of our group from that trip. I can imagine that photo as
though it were from my own memory, of the girls, our arms around
one another, the smiles. This friend I'd forgotten is the one, in fact,
who brought back into my memory this year that began with this
trip into the woods, a year that I still call the worst year of my life, a
year when my home life spun out of my control, when I was bullied
extensively by a few kids, one girl in particular, when my under-
standing of girls and their power formed, and a year that I somehow pushed from my memory so that I could not fully recover it.

Ashley

WHEN ASHLEY AND I FINISHED ELEMENTARY AND MOVED on to Horace Mann for seventh grade, she sat with Tiffany and her friends during lunch and seemed to forget that she and I had been friends first. The popular girls laughed with her, so easy. Okay, I thought. Easy. And I bought my sandwich and my bottle of juice and I made my way over. But as soon as I sat next to Ashley I could feel the shift of energy, the stares.

"Hey," Ashley said. She looked at her new friends. "This is Kerry."

Half smiles, cocked heads. Tiffany and two others didn't even do that.

"Cory!" Tiffany called out to a boy, cute, in a white polo and jeans. "Aren't you going to sit?"

He slid in next to her. We met eyes a moment.

"This is Ashley," Tiffany said, "And Lisa."

I took a sip of juice, pushed the sandwich away. A white wall of noise began to form in my head, louder and louder, so that their voices sounded far away, as though they were on one side of a tunnel and I was on the other. I stayed there like that, watching my hands, for the rest of the period. Finally, it was over and I walked quickly out of the cafeteria toward my next class.

In the mornings, my mother chatted and laughed with Tyler, the one she related to more, the one who shielded her from hard feelings, the one who took her side when our father moved out. I focused on gathering my things for the hour-and-a-half ride to our school in New York. The bus driver was a physical education teacher who lived in New Jersey, too, and made extra money using this van that had five rows of seats. He honked from the end of the driveway at exactly 7:05, and then we followed the same route each day to pick up the other seven Jersey kids, including Ashley. Ashley sat next to me, but when we arrived at school and stepped down off the bus into the area in front of the breezeway, Tiffany and her friends whisked Ashley away, leaving me alone.

At the lockers I saw Ashley. Her new friends were there, laughing and flipping hair. One girl tucked in her friend's tag. She was short with curly blond hair. I think her name was Suzy. Another was tall and skinny with freckles. She was my sort-of friend in elementary school, but she didn't acknowledge me now.

"Ashley?"

She didn't hear me. Someone else had yelled something and she was laughing with the others.

"Ashley?" I said it louder.

She turned. "Oh, hey. I didn't see you there."

"Want to walk to first period together?"

"Sure. Give me a minute."

I went to sit against the radiator on the other wall to wait. I could feel the heat seeping through my jeans to the back of my thighs. I watched as Ashley laughed with her friends. Minutes passed—five, then ten. And then she walked off with those girls toward the stairs. If I focus my mind's eye I can imagine myself there, my brown bangs hanging into my eyes, my backpack leaning against my leg. The world thins down to just me, alone, without an ally.

After that year, I changed schools, and Ashley and I lost touch. In eleventh grade, though, Ashley and I ran into each another, and she was eager to start up our friendship again. She said things like, "You were always so fun that way..." Or, "I always loved how you..." and I wondered if I remembered us wrong, if that girl on the radiator was just a fantasy I'd made up, if I was just always determined to be on the outside, desperate for connection.

Tiffany

WHEN YOU STAND AT THE ENTRANCE TO HORACE MANN you see a breezeway separating two buildings. Hickories and hemlock trees line the street. To the left are the cafeteria and auditorium. To the right is a four-story stone structure, the Katz Library and Tillinghast Hall, built in the 1920s and renovated in the 1950s, with a wide wooden stairway leading to the halls of classrooms and the library. Walk beneath the breezeway and before you is a long expanse of grass, the main field. Follow the walkway to the right, past the old building, and you come upon the newer science building, Pforzheimer Hall, and then Fisher Hall, the arts building. Go past this to the left and you are at the Prettyman Gym and Pool, behind which are tennis courts. Across the street is another sports field. An insular campus of privilege and wealth.

Slowly these images come back, come into focus like photos developing, the edges and colors sharpening, the smells of fresh cut grass and fallen leaves, the floor wax and wood polish on the banister along those stairs. I see the lockers and the lined books in the library, the kids with their backpacks and loafers and turtlenecks. I smell the gymnasium, the rubber and sweat, hear the squeak of sneakers. I can feel the rough texture of the stone, the sensation of the soft grass in my fingers as I nervously pull it from the field. And the emotions, too. They come in, winding their way through my body from some ancient place—the embarrassment, the loneliness, the sense of being barely there.

I sat in my first class in Tillinghast, first floor. Spanish class.

Gaby was in there, and also Tiffany. The teacher, Mrs. Durso, called out each of our names, and I filed them in my mind, repeating them to myself like a mantra—Kylie, Jeff, Jason, Gaby, Cory, Marion, Tiffany, Courtney, Lionel, Joe. When she said my name I nodded, but she didn't see. She looked up from her paper and lowered the glasses from her face.

"Kerry?" she said again, scanning the class.

"Here," I said, my face turning red. A few students turned to look at me. I felt Tiffany's gaze.

Mrs. Durso moved on, but I still felt conspicuous, too big.

At dismissal I slid my notebook and pen into my backpack. The kids around me had LeSportsac bags. They wore Guess jeans and Polo. Their hair was curled and sprayed, their skin scrubbed and pimple free. These kids were ridiculously rich. Their fathers were the CEOs of Merrill Lynch and the Gap, corporate lawyers, and neurosurgeons. My family was rich, too, but not like that. Not filthy rich. I had to wear my sister's hand-me-downs, and my mother only bought us our designer clothes on sale. I used Sea Breeze, while they used Clinique. I scrubbed my face with St. Ives, while they had concoctions made up especially for their skin from their mothers' spas on Fifth Avenue. The night before this first day of seventh grade I'd called my friend Liz on the phone to plan what we'd wear. She remembers to this day that I wore a red and yellow striped Ralph Lauren Polo shirt with matching red pants. She remembers that I wore mascara, something she couldn't even fathom. Liz and I wouldn't see each other much at Horace Mann because her mother had encouraged her to branch out and make new friends who weren't from our elementary school. My own mother made no such admonishments. She gave me no guidance at all, in fact, caught up as she was in her own despair about my father's affair and leaving. I felt lost and alone, flung from the safety of one school to another that was too big, too wealthy, too unfamiliar.

I opened the door to the music room. Inside there were tables pushed up against the wall, piled with violin cases, drum kit pieces, drum sticks, stacks of compositions. The middle of the room was crowded with black metal music stands and folding metal chairs. A few kids were in there—one putting a flute together, reed in mouth; one tuning a guitar. I had my drum pad in my backpack, but I didn't move to unzip it. These were the sorts of kids who only showered once a week, on whom puberty looked like a bad mistake, their faces greasy and pimpled, their feet too big for their lanky bodies. In elementary school everyone played an instrument, including the well-liked kids. Especially them. I started off with flute but then switched to percussion when my best friend started in that section. I had been in band, orchestra, and chamber choir. I had taken pride in it. When I was given the choice of an elective art, I instinctively checked band. It didn't occur to me that I'd be the only one, that everyone else was taking photography and theater—how could I have been so stupid!—the cooler arts.

"Welcome. What do you play?" the greasy one with the reed in his mouth asked. He grinned, revealing a row of braces.

"Nothing," I said, stepping backward and reaching for the door. "Wrong room."

Later, I stepped off the bus near my house. I was the last drop-off. It was almost five o'clock in the evening. That's how long it took to get home, after dropping off the other New Jersey kids on our bus. And Tyler was taking a late bus home because she played field hockey after school. It was my mother's idea for us to go so far for school. She believed that an education at a place like Horace Mann was essential for our futures. I waved goodbye to the driver and walked along the gravel road that led to our house. We lived in Harrington Park, a suburban town about twenty minutes from the George Washington Bridge. My house was one of four houses off a gravel drive, tucked away inside a small patch of woods, right next to the railroad tracks. On weekends I rode my bike down the road and on to the street that led to the main artery in town. There was the train station, the corner store, the hardware store, and the market. There was also a bank at the bottom of a hill I liked to charge by on my bike. I rode past these to the residential streets, past houses of people I didn't know. There were lots of kids in our town, and I passed them too as they played out on the road or in the front yards of their homes. They all went to the public high school. I didn't mean to be ungrateful. I knew my father was paying a fortune so my mother would get what she wanted, for us girls to get this sort of education. It's just that I never seemed to belong anywhere, not here in my hometown, not at the fancy prep school I attended.

The gravel crunched beneath my shoes. I passed our front yard first, which was surrounded by a wide moat of ivy. Two ancient maples hovered in the yard, then the mass of oaks and hemlocks by the driveway. I followed the driveway to the back door and turned the knob. It was locked. I dropped my knapsack and crouched down to search for my keys. I always forgot them, and today was no different. I rang the doorbell, but my mother's van wasn't there. She was in class forty-five minutes away, studying pre-med. This was the year she would take her MCATs, get her applications in, and … and what? I didn't yet know, couldn't yet imagine, or couldn't yet understand that my mother would leave the country for medical school and that Tyler and I would move in with our father, and everything, everything would change. I didn't know. All I knew was that in this moment I was locked out of my house, and that I was hungry and exhausted from the day.

I left my bag there and went into the front yard, where there was a Japanese maple I liked to climb. I got to the second row of branches, my loafers slipping the whole way, and looked up at the fading light through the purple leaves. So much of what I remember is just like this—myself alone, with no witnesses to my life. I stayed in that tree for two hours, my stomach hollow with hunger, until finally I heard the rumbling of a bus, my sister, who always had her keys, who shook her head at me, *what is wrong with you?*

I don't know. I don't know what is wrong with me.

And soon after, Tiffany determined that there really was something wrong with me.

"What's that you're doing with your head?" she asked.

"What?"

We were outside after school, waiting for out buses to arrive. "Do you see that?" she asked Courtney, who peered back at me. "How she's shaking her head?" Ashley was nearby too. Just a moment ago she had been talking with Tiffany and Courtney, but now she didn't hear. Or she acted as though she didn't hear. "What are you talking about?" I said, but I could hear how soft my voice was compared to hers. I held my head as still as I could. Was it shaking without my knowing?

She shook her head, little tremors. Her curly hair lifted slightly in the breeze. I was wearing my new miniskirt, the same one Courtney had on, but mine was blue and hers was red. Courtney laughed, watching Tiffany imitate me.

From that day forward, almost every time I passed Tiffany, Courtney, and a few of the boys, they did that shaking thing with their heads. At home I stood before the mirror in my bedroom watching for whatever it was they'd seen. It never happened while I was looking, or if it did I couldn't see it. I spent hours there, simply examining my head, watching for shaking. Tremors. I put on makeup. I tried putting my hair up, then shook it back out.There was something about me, I was learning. There were things about me I couldn't see. Ugly things. Things I couldn't control.

My mother set up a dartboard on the sun porch. It said MCAT in her large calligraphy-like letters. She thought that people would think that was funny, that they'd admire her lighthearted approach to this difficult thing she was doing. My grandparents visited often to stay with us so my mother could go to hotels and retreats to study. When my grandmother caught me sulking, she told me, "Your mother is doing something amazing, especially after your father's shenanigans. Don't make this unnecessarily hard for her." It was a warning more than anything else. Don't you dare put your feelings before your mother's.

At night I heard my mother in her room, working at her desk. She painstakingly copied definitions and drew colored pencil illustrations of cells and dermis layers and organs. I snuck in

there when she wasn't around to see. Her notebook pages were like works of art. Strange, alien creatures—an artery broken down by layer, a neuron and its electrical impulse. I ran my fingers over the slight ridges of the paper, knowing that this was where her mind was now. This unknowable world would be her life.

At school I saw Andrew and Tiffany coming from the other end of the breezeway. I had developed a sharp vision for her, so I could steel myself against what was coming. I readjusted my backpack, always over just one shoulder. That was the rule. Only dorks wore it on both. I looked down so we wouldn't meet eyes, watched the cement, the smudges from scuffed sneakers. I tried to breathe, breathe, breathe. Just get through this moment, and then the next.

A push against my arm then. Hard. I stumbled against the wooden fence that surrounded the field. Hit it hard but uprighted myself quickly before too many people saw.

"Watch it, Tremors," Andrew said. He's the one who pushed me. "If you'd stop shaking your head like that you could maybe walk straight."

Then Tiffany's harsh, raspy laugh.

In Mr. White's history class, before he showed up, Liz stopped me.

"How are you?" she asked. Her eyes were warm and blue. She wore no makeup, still wore her hair straight and flat against her head like she had since fourth grade. We had been so close, but now I didn't know her. Or, I didn't know how to know her.

"I'm great," I said. "Really great."

"You just ... you seem like you're not okay."

"I am." I sat down, started rifling through my backback for my book.

"I heard about your mom," she said.

"Heard what about my mom?" My throat was tight. I didn't dare look at her.

"Medical school. That's really amazing."

I didn't speak. So many *didn't*s. All the negative space, the shrinking away, the disappearing that happens to girls at this age. Then, Mr. White walked in, his heavy belly above his khakis, his knit tie.

"I have a boyfriend now," I whispered to Liz.

Her expression lit up. "Really?"

"I meet him on my bike. He lives in my town."

"Wow," she said. She pointed to my eyes. "I guess the mascara worked."

"Maybe you should try it sometime," I told her.

The phone rang during dinner and my mother jumped up. She wasn't one of those mothers who believed we should focus on one another while we ate. If someone wanted her, she was desperate to know. We ate in front of the television, anyway, at the bar-height butcher-block table that was pushed up against the wall. The news was on. 1982. Princess Grace had died when her car plunged off a mountain road. Her seventeen-year-old daughter sustained injuries, but certainly no injuries worse than the fact that her mother had died.

"It's for you," my mother said. She handed me the phone, clear disappointment on her face.

My sister raised her eyebrows. She wasn't popular at Horace Mann. She kept to herself and her small group of mousy friends.

But she also didn't care about popularity at all. Somewhere along the line I'd told her I was popular, and now I needed to keep up the lie. I took the phone.

"Hello?" My voice quiet, hesitant.

"Is this Kerry?"

"Yes."

"Do you have the math homework?" I heard muffled sounds.

"Who is this?" I could feel my mother and sister eyeing me.

"It's your best friends." More muffled sounds. Giggling.

My face grew hot. I didn't have best friends at Horace Mann.

"Who is this?" I said again.

"It's shaky and shivery." Explosive laughter. I hurled myself forward and slammed the phone down in its cradle.

"Well?" my mother said.

"Wrong number."

Later, I borrowed my mother's typewriter and wrote notes from my boyfriend on slips of paper.

> I can't wait to see you again. You are beautiful.
> Love, Jason

> I like you so much. I think about you all the time.
> Love, Jason.

In bed that night I imagined there really was a boyfriend. He met me in those woods and we kissed. He told me I was beautiful and that he'd been waiting for me his whole life. Me too, I told him. My sister was in my mother's bedroom, the door ajar. They were discussing something about my mother. They often did. Some concern my mother had about our father and his treatment of us. My sister soothing her, telling her it was all going to be okay.

CHILDREN CAN BELIEVE themselves so clever. Shaky and Shivery. Almost daily I recived written notes from them, my new best friends. Tiffany and her partners slipped them into my locker, my backpack, my jean pockets when I changed for gym.

Dear Tremors,

You are my best friend in the whole world. Please don't ever stop moving your head in that weird way you do.

All my love,

Shaky

Dear Tremors,

Let's always walk around looking stupid together.

Love and kisses,

Shivery

I crumpled the notes in my fist and dropped them in the garbage cans around campus. I should have burned them. I should have saved them. I would have them today to send to Tiffany, to say *Look at what you did to me.* To ask her why. To show her my accomplishments now. To show her that my head doesn't shake, that it never shook, that I still have no idea what she and Andrew were talking about. To shame her. I'd want to shame her with them. Maybe she'd think about how cruel this was. Maybe she has kids and would imagine someone treating them this way. Maybe she'd apologize. But I threw them out quickly, eager to get them away from me, to disconnect, to begin the long process of denial. This didn't happen. It didn't. I'm fine.

As adults, Gaby told me that her own memory of Tiffany was that she was an outsider, a wannabe. Nobody actually took her seriously. I go to her Facebook page and see her. Still her. The broad face and nose. The thin, curly blond hair. I think she's a therapist or runs a nonprofit or something. I don't see any partners or children. In truth, she looks a little sad and lonely. But that could just be something I need to believe about her. A few times I think about contacting her, asking her why she treated me the way she did. I can see she's just a woman, just a person. But I'm too scared. Still. Still scared of the me from back then, how she created me, like Frankenstein. A girl who believed I was a monster and not worthy of anything better.

I have just one photo from that year; it was taken later that fall. I stand against the stone wall on the edge of the Main Field. I wear my blue Cutter & Buck jacket, my hands in my pockets, a buttondown shirt beneath a V-neck sweater. My hair is shoulder length, pulled back from my bangs with a barrette. I am almost smiling, but not quite. More like a pained smirk. And my eyes look dark and sad. I showed my seven-year-old son the photo, and he said, "That's you? It doesn't look like you at all."

But it was. It was me.

Laura

MY MOTHER AND SISTER AND I SPENT OUR CHRISTMAS vacations in the Berkshires, where my grandparents had a condominium. They went to Florida in the cold months, and we drove the three and a half hours up there to ski. We used to go with my father, but now it was just the three of us. They knew us at the mountain and at the small antique shops we browsed after days of skiing. The snow piled fifteen feet high at the sides of the road and in the parking lot of the Grand Union, where we shopped.

This winter my mother announced we'd be going with her new boyfriend, Arthur, who looked like a giant gnome. He was stocky and thick, and he had a long white beard. My mother told Tyler and me that we could each bring a friend. Tyler chose Laura, with brown greasy hair and glasses. And I chose Ashley, but Ashley couldn't come. At this point, Tiffany had already begun teasing me about the phantom movement I made with my head, the slight shake I didn't even know that I did. But I was learning that there were things like this about me, ugly things, things I couldn't control. I was sure that's why Ashley couldn't make it. She didn't want anyone to think we were actual friends.

So, when it was time to leave for western Massachusetts, I went without a friend. During the days I threw myself into skiing. I challenged myself with black diamond slopes, with moguls, and in the evenings I listened to music in the basement bedroom.

My mother asked me to get a certain set of wine glasses from

the dining room cabinet, but I got the wrong ones—red instead of white. When I brought another set, those were wrong too. "I'll do it," Tyler said, and she somehow found what my mother wanted. They were always on the same wavelength that way. "I'll just have to buy Kerry a guide to wine glasses," my mother said, and they laughed. When she saw my expression she added, "Oh, come on, Kerry. You don't have a sense of humor."

One evening, I heard Laura and Tyler arguing. And then Laura came stomping down the stairs. She sat angrily on the bed where I lay. "Tyler is such an idiot!" she said. From here I could see the way her freckles covered her entire face. They went all the way down her arms too. I felt briefly defensive of my sister, but only briefly. "Okay if I hang out with you for a little bit?"

I shrugged. I didn't connect with Laura, but I'd been lonely this entire vacation. I was always lonely in my mother's world.

We arrived upstairs together in time for dinner. Tyler sat with her head turned. Only once I pulled my chair up to the table did she give me a look.

"What?" I asked.

Laura smiled. "Yeah, what?"

Tyler didn't answer. She looked down at her meal, pushed her food around. My mother was too busy with Arthur to notice anything.

Laura and I spent the rest of the vacation together. We skied. Browsed the shops. Laughed at people. Tyler kept her distance. Sometimes she examined us, her expression thick with hurt. I didn't even like Laura all that much. But it was a relief to have someone to hang around with when my mother was there. It was a relief to be able to be myself, even if it meant that Tyler had to feel bad. Wasn't this how it always was with us? With our father I was comfortable and she withdrew. With our mother she was relaxed and I went mute. It was always either her or me. We could never both have what we wanted.

Back at school, Laura saw me in the hallway. She called my name, but I walked fast in the other direction. I wasn't interested in being her friend now that we were back to real life.

Elisabeth

WE LIKED TO SAY WE WERE WOMB SISTERS. OUR MOTH-
ers met when they were pregnant with us, but we didn't become
friends until we were thirteen. My mother and father had just
divorced, and my mother was suddenly like an alien. Sometimes I
came home to find her crying. Other times I found her hard at work
on some house project, such as laying two tons of bluestone on
the patio. My father's apartment was another unfamiliar place, lit-
tered with ashtrays and video games and loud music, with women
I didn't know smelling of perfume and slinking through rooms in
nothing but robes.

I went to Elisabeth's to escape, to sink into her world. A safer
world. But also a wild, vivid one. Elisabeth was like no one I'd ever
known. She painted abstracts on an easel in her bedroom, Sting
on the record player. She yelled and cried about her mother's alco-
holism and her stepfather's abuse. She laughed loudly and with
abandon. She stole cigarettes and we smoked them by the creek
behind her house, and then we snuck out at night to go meet boys
she would make out with but I wouldn't.

In the fall, my mother began to talk about medical school,
and I couldn't imagine yet what this meant—that she would leave
Tyler and me to study abroad, and Tyler and I would move in with
our father, and everything, everything would be different.

I started at a new school, where a girl named Trish picked up
on my sadness and teased me until I grew small and worthless and
concealed. On the weekends, Elisabeth came over, and we made

up dance moves and she hugged me and said, "I love you so much!" and I pretended I was still real and alive and whole. I didn't tell any of my new friends about Elisabeth, afraid they would think her too wild, too exposed, too raw. I started a process of burying myself that I'd continue for a long, long time. I started a process of denying and shape shifting, eager for the approval of others.

When my mother left for good, right before the summer, Tyler and I picked out paint colors for our new rooms with my father. I chose hot pink. Tyler chose blue. We didn't speak of what was happening. We avoided each other's eyes. It would be a long time before we would come back together again. Meanwhile, I begged my father to take me out of the school where Trish was and to let me attend the local public school. I wanted to start anew. I wanted to be anyone but me.

Before my new school started, I shopped for clothes that matched the girls' there. Concert tees and tight Guess jeans and chain belts. I feathered my hair. I wore heavy eye makeup. Elisabeth didn't understand who this new me was. She yelled at me, I yelled back, and then we were no longer friends. She called on the phone to talk to my sister, and with my heart in my throat I shouted out for my sister to come get the phone.

Years later, as adults, Elisabeth and I reconnected, and we finally discussed what had happened that summer. I told her how hurt I'd been, and she told me that that's not what happened at all. "Don't you remember?" she said. "You dropped *me*. You stopped talking to me, and I was heartbroken."

How fascinating memory is, how astounding the stories we tell, how those stories swirl with our grief and become their very own things, precious to us, and intractable.

Kelly

BOYS LIKED KELLY, AND I KNEW THAT WELL. SHE WAS CUTE and blond with a shapely body at only thirteen. We shared clothes, a pair of Guess jeans that had a row of buttons at the crotch, a shirt that showed off her cleavage, but sagged on my small chest. She lived in a small, dirty house on the other side of town with her parents, sister, cousin, and her cousin's boyfriend. They all shared one bathroom. She had a boyfriend who lived two towns over, and we'd get her cousin to drive us there. We hung out in a park, waiting for her boyfriend to show up, and then we walked about a mile to his house. She disappeared with her boyfriend into his bedroom for hours while I watched television. Once, a boy named Iggy was there. I'd heard he sniffed glue when he couldn't find any other drugs. He wore a worn-in leather jacket and he smelled unclean and like cigarette and pot smoke. His face was pockmarked and scarred, and he was ugly. But one afternoon I let him put his fingers inside me on Kelly's boyfriend's couch. I jerked him off, my first time touching a penis, and then we sat awkwardly until Kelly and her boyfriend came back out and we could leave. Eventually they did, and Kelly pulled me aside to tell me she and her boyfriend had 69ed. She giggled and put her arm through mine as the four of us made our way back to the park, as if I were just like her, as if we belonged together. I didn't tell her about Iggy, about how his tongue had tasted sour, how his fingers had hurt as he pushed them clumsily inside me. Kelly had no idea what it would be like to be me, the less pretty one, the one who boys never liked. Only

boys like Iggy, and even Iggy walked ahead of us, unconcerned with me now. In a shoebox under her bed, Kelly kept memorabilia about her dead friend. Laurie, who had lived on the Jersey shore. Laurie with thick black curls. The most beautiful girl who ever lived. That's what Kelly said. She said, "I'll never love anyone the way I loved Laurie." She said that right to my face. Laurie had been killed by a drunk driver at fourteen. The whole town where she'd lived loved her. Her boyfriend slept on her grave for nine days before the city finally made him leave. In the shoebox were photos, a dirty braided rope bracelet, peace sign earrings, scribbled notes, a doodle of two dogs, and ticket stubs to movies I'd never seen. I sifted through the magical box unsure where I fit into Kelly's life until she told me to stop touching her special things.

In the summer, Kelly's cousin drove us out to visit Laurie's grave. I didn't want to go, didn't want to have to act sad about someone I didn't know, whom I didn't even think I liked. My nemesis. That's who that dead girl was. But I awkwardly rubbed Kelly's back while she stood by Laurie's grave and cried. We stood there a long time, until I slowly began to disappear, until we were two ghosts and one whole girl.

Chris

STACY'S FAVORITE SONG WAS "TAINTED LOVE." SHE
played it over and over on her cassette player. Her favorite color
was purple. And she called herself boy crazy, even though we were
only eleven. We shared a cabin at Northway Camp, an all-girls camp
at Algonquin Park in Ontario, Canada. We bathed in the morning
by jumping into the freezing lake. We screamed, pulled ourselves
out, lathered up, and then jumped back in, laughing and screaming some more. We went to the fifties dance dressed as boyfriend
and girlfriend. I was the boy. I auditioned to be Annie in the camp
play, and I got the part. I could sing pretty well, and I was good. I
remember I was good.

There was an older girl, Chris. I think she was fourteen. That's
who this story is really about. She played guitar and sang. She wore
destroyed jeans and had long, straight blond hair. She smelled like
some sort of flower, roses or lilies. I can almost smell it now. She let
Stacy and me sit on her lap, called us to her. She thought we were
so cute. She braided our hair before camp dances and brought us
little gifts: leaves and rocks she found in the forest. Bracelets she
wove. Tiny dolls she had sewn. I must have been ten years old then
because my parents were still together, and I had no sense of the
world as anything other than soft and receptive. Sometimes it's
hard to put time in the right order, and then take it apart piece by
piece. I was ten, or I was eleven. Only recently did I ask my mother
outright when she and my father separated, and I was shocked to

find out I was ten at the time. And here, all along, I remembered being eleven. Memory is a slippery eel.

When Stacy and I left each other that summer, we hugged and cried and promised to stay in touch. We wrote back and forth two letters total in our rounded, preteen lettering, hearts over the *i*s. I don't remember who wrote last. I don't remember, I don't remember. But somewhere in the next year or two I changed into someone else. I got a perm. I did drugs. I got boy crazy, too, but not in a cute, young girl way. My desire for boys was tinged with desperation. Grown-up needs. Tainted love. My mother had left to go to medical school in another country, and I lived with my father and sister in a new home in a new town in a new world.

Near the end of my eighth-grade year, I had a party in my father's apartment. He was away on business. My best friend Kelly came, and all of our friends too. And then some people I didn't know, and then some men in their early twenties who stole my father's drugs and a gun and the small appliances in boxes waiting to be installed in the kitchen renovation. My father was furious. He was also terrified. What was happening to his little girl? So he made me go to work with him every day, and then he signed me up for Northway Camp for the month of August.

I arrived at the airport in Canada, and then we took the bus to the boat that would motor us to the camp. I recognized most of the other campers, but they didn't recognize me. Stacy wasn't there, but Chris was. She was a counselor-in-training now. I approached her, excited. I hadn't realized until that moment that I longed for her. Not for her exactly, but for someone to take me onto her lap again, to braid my hair, to treat me like the child I still was somewhere inside. But she didn't even say hello.

That was the summer I befriended another girl whose name I can't remember because no one else was interested in me quite as much as she was. She was a counselor-in-training also, and older than me. She told me she was a witch. We rolled Drum tobacco into cigarettes and put spells on boys we liked back home. We took photos or pictures from magazines and meditated on the images. We sent messages with our thoughts. It was almost like praying. God, I wanted it to work. I wanted so much to believe I had control. That I could stop the world from spinning out from under me, that I could have something I wanted. But not one boy liked me. Not for at least a few more years. And, anyway, this is a story about girls.

Chrissy

I STARTED EIGHTH GRADE AT THE LOCAL PUBLIC SCHOOL. I had bought the concert tees and the chain belt and the bandana to tie around my thigh. I bought the Def Leppard album and the perm and the Iron Maiden patch for my jacket. But when I took the bus that first day and then walked into the school halls I saw that making friends would not come easy. Everyone was already grouped together: the cool kids, the less cool kids, and the even less cool. They didn't even notice me. None of them did. Except Chrissy. Chrissy was tall and skinny. She had a big nose and tiny eyes, and she wore a short, feathered hairdo that belonged on someone much older.

She asked, "Are you new?"

We were in English class together, and it had just ended. I nodded, my stomach sinking. I wanted to make friends, but she wasn't who I would have chosen. I knew, even then, how unfair and selfish that was, but I wanted so much to be taken in by the right group. I wanted to be made worthwhile by them. But they weren't aware of me, and Chrissy was, so when she asked me to hang out after school I said yes.

Chrissy and I spent lots of time together in those first few weeks of school. Our conversations were halting. They bored me. We didn't see things the same way. She was much more conservative. Her humor wasn't funny to me. I longingly watched the girls I'd come to know as the cool kids: Stephanie, Jackie, Hayley, and Lisa. I believed they'd like me if they just got to know me, if they didn't think Chrissy and I were really friends. When they were around, I stayed away from Chrissy. I tried to look ready to be picked. I wore my headphones and listened to their music. I hummed along, hoping they'd hear.

It was only a few weeks later that they began to talk to me here and there. First Stephanie, because we waited at the same bus stop, then Hayley. Not Lisa. Not yet. And it was around this same time that Chrissy told me that she suddenly had a boyfriend. He told her she was pretty, she explained, and he said he liked her so much all he could do was think about her. He lived in Palisades Park, and she took the bus to see him sometimes. Did I want to come? I didn't know anyone yet who had a boyfriend. That world: the world of boys and their attention and all the ways that would come to control my life—that world had not yet begun for me. But, I said I'd go because she pleaded with me, and I knew she had seen me talking with Stephanie and Hayley. I knew she could feel the way I'd begun to recede, clarifying for her, in ways she surely couldn't identify at the time, in ways that she probably struggled with for many, many years as she grew, that she was a placeholder for me and nothing more.

Chrissy and I rode on the bus together to Palisades Park. I don't remember what we talked about or how things were between us. I only remember standing in the crisp early November air outside his house. The house was nestled inside a circle of trees, and the lawn was scattered with dead leaves. Chrissy rang the doorbell. Then she knocked. Then she rang the doorbell again. We waited on the lawn, crunching leaves beneath our high tops, chatting about I don't remember what. After awhile we made our way back to the bus stop and headed back to our town. It occurred to me, for the first time, that Chrissy didn't have a boyfriend. That she had her own sly way of getting by in a place where she wasn't noticed either.

The next day, she approached me while I spoke with Stephanie. I saw her coming and tried to turn away. I tried to pretend I didn't know her.

"My boyfriend called last night," she said.

Stephanie stared at her, but she didn't look at Stephanie. She only looked at me. "He said he was taking a nap and didn't hear us."

Us. I looked at Stephanie for feedback, hoping she wasn't going to turn on me now that she knew Chrissy and I had spent time together. "Oh," I said. I just wanted her to leave.

"He said you were kind of fat."

My blood froze. I said nothing. I felt nothing. I clenched one of my hands into a fist and dug my nails into my palm.

"Just wanted to tell you," she said and walked away.

As soon as she was gone, Stephanie breathed out a laugh. "Who would be her boyfriend?" she said. "She's so ugly. And that hair."

"Yeah," I said. "I know."

"Did you see what he looked like?" she asked. "Who is he to call you fat?"

I leaned in close to her. "Honestly? I don't think she even has a boyfriend. I think she made the whole thing up."

Stephanie covered her mouth and laughed, her eyes wide. "Oh, my God, what a loser!" she said.

I laughed with her. But I still sometimes wonder what became of Chrissy. And, even though no one ever called me fat again, I still believe I am.

Maureen

MAUREEN LIVED IN THE APARTMENTS ACROSS FROM mine. To get to her bedroom you had to walk through her older brother's bedroom. She had no father. I had no mother. Or at least we felt that was the case. We set our sights on boys, as would become my story. I still hadn't found one who I liked who also liked me. She was sexier than I was, had an adult movement in her hips that suggested she knew more than she should, that I recognize now as evidence of her having grown through something already she shouldn't have.

We didn't speak much while at school. People thought of her as a slut, and I didn't want to be associated with her. It was unkind, I know. But I would be unkind in this particular way many more times before I stopped blaming others for the ways things fell apart in my friendships. I would have to confess to my faults, to my neediness, to my selfishness in order to learn how to have good friendships. For now, though, I was too young and self-unaware.

After school my friends and I hung out at the Burger King down the street. There was a guy behind the counter who met my eyes many times. He reminded me of Prince. I had just watched *Purple Rain*, and I had never seen that sort of heated romance before. I wanted that. I wanted to feel something, anything other than the endless grief about my mother's abandonment.

So Maureen and I went there one evening and invited him to her house. I have no idea where I told my father I was or whether he cared. The Prince guy showed up two hours later, and we put on

Purple Rain, the album, and he and I started dancing. He kissed me, using his tongue. He had no idea I was only fourteen. He moved his hands along my back, up to my bra. He kissed my neck. He said, "Come on," referring to Maureen's bedroom. I shook my head, scared.

"Come on," he said. "I want to be with you."

I shook my head again, and he pushed me away.

"What the hell?" he said. "You invited me over here!"

"I know," I said, not sure how to explain.

"Fuck you," he said. "Fucking little tease is what you are."

Maureen was in the other room dancing by herself. He passed her on his way out, and I heard him say, "I should have hooked up with you instead. You would have followed through."

She said nothing, and I don't know how she reacted, whether she was insulted or pleased, or angry for me. I don't know. What I do know is that this was the day I learned two things: that I was utterly replaceable, that I could disappear just like that, like I did for my mother; and that if I wanted to be worth attention, if I wanted to matter to anyone, I had better give them something in return.

The door shut and I came out to where she was.

"You okay?" she asked.

I nodded.

I don't remember how our friendship ended. Unlike so many of my friends, I don't think there was much emotion attached to it. I think we just faded away into our separate lives. But I think of her sometimes, and that she didn't judge what I did, while I stood by and let others judge her.

Miesha

MIESHA CALLED MY FATHER BIRD. SHE WAS FOURTEEN years old, but she just walked into our living room and said, "Hey, Bird." We cut school together and got high with my dad's weed, lying on my bedroom floor with Pink Floyd on the record player. We smoked cigarettes in the stairwell of my tenth-floor apartment and drew pictures and silly comments that meant nothing to anyone but us. I don't know where my father was. Probably at work. I was often left alone, left to do what I wanted, and what I wanted was to fuck off from life. The stairwell always smelled like stale cigarette smoke, and it was our fault. We didn't care. We didn't care about anything but our own fun.

Miesha lived in a house on the other side of town with her two older brothers, her mentally unstable mother, and her quiet, unassuming father. Her brothers dressed up in army fatigues and snuck around the neighborhood working up schemes. They played paintball and other war games I had no interest in. Mostly they ignored Miesha and me, who were only annoying to them.

Once, we were in her living room watching *Woody Woodpecker*. She had a boyfriend and often, she confessed to me, watched *Woody Woodpecker* while they had sex. "What?" she said when I laughed. "If he were any good maybe I'd, you know, *not* watch TV instead." *Woody Woodpecker*. Right? It was too good. Anyway, we were in her living room one afternoon on a Saturday and her moth-

er came downstairs wearing a nightgown and a fur coat and big, heavy rain boots.

She said, "Hurry, get my keys! Your father and brothers are trying to kill me!"

"Dad's not home, Mom," Miesha said. She looked at me and did that whirly thing with her finger next to her ear, meaning, my mother is banana crackers.

"Don't do that, young lady!" her mother said. She was so tiny. She had thin, short blond hair and big glasses. The coat swallowed her. "I'm not crazy," she said. "I'm being bludgeoned!" She held out one leg and then the other, pulling up her nightgown as she did. "See? See?" There was nothing there, of course, but her pale skin, her veins blue beneath.

Miesha sighed and called her father, who arrived an hour later and escorted her to the mental hospital. Miesha seemed unfazed, and later we invited over her boyfriend and a few of his friends. That night a boy I liked fingered me, and then he became my boyfriend.

Miesha and I befriended two other boys, sophomores, who were funny as shit. They made us a tape, not of music, but of ridiculous improvisational songs and conversations. One started like this: *Oh my fish, my fishy fish. How I love you. How I love you, fishy fish.* They were stupid and nonsensical, and we loved them.

Then we went to high school. Ninth grade. And Miesha started hanging out with Elissa, who was beautiful and mean, and who one day said outright to me, "She's mine now, so you might as well give up." With a broken heart, I did.

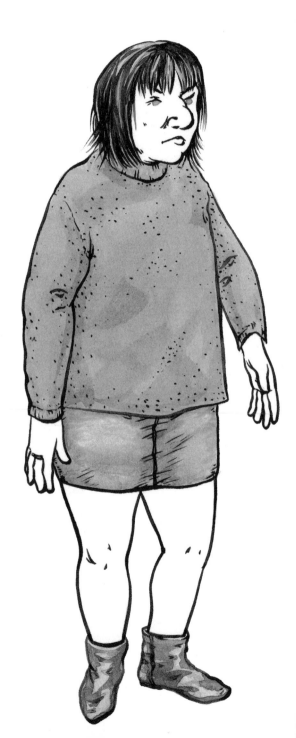

Amy

EVERYONE AT THE NEW SCHOOL SEEMED UNATTAINABLE. I walked with my gaze down, afraid to be seen, afraid to not be seen. I wore the clothes I'd seen on the kids when I did a tour. I was always in costume in this way. I spotted the popular girls right away. They were always so easy to spot—laughing, heads thrown back, walking arm in arm through the hallways. Boys turned their heads as they passed. If anyone was truly unattainable, it was those girls. Amy spotted me one day between buildings. What must I have looked like to her? The new girl, the girl with no place? She homed in on me, matching my pace.

"You're new?" she asked.

I nodded.

"Did you just move here?"

"I got in trouble at my other school, so my dad made me come here," I told her.

"In trouble for what?"

"Boys," I said, and her eyes lit up.

Amy had a Honda Accord, so she drove us into Manhattan every weekend to go to bars. This was when you could flash your fake ID to the smirking bouncer, who simply waved us in. We were girls, after all, and girls were always welcome. Our favorite bar was Dorrian's Red Hand, which was full of boys in sports jackets with their school crests sewn onto them, their ties loosened, and beautiful girls who wore heels and tight dresses. In the bathroom, we all did cocaine off the tank of the toilets, the stall door

locked. We drank sea breezes and sex on the beaches and grape-
fruit vodkas. Our parents were always gone, in St. Martens or Los
Angeles, playing golf or wheeling deals. They left us stacks of hun-
dred-dollar bills on the granite kitchen counters so we could buy
ourselves food. One man, who was twenty-one and just finish-
ing at Columbia, brought me home to his parents' brownstone in
Greenwich Village. Another boy, fifteen and wily, a boy who knew
the bouncer that night, made out with me in the booth in the corner. Every night, Amy and I sat at our table and prayed for boys to
find us there.

When we got back to my apartment in New Jersey, it was
two or four in the morning. While my father slept, we made Kraft
macaroni and cheese and watched *Kojak*, the only program on that
time of night. The next night, we did it all over again. Soon we were
going in on school nights. I was always late the next day. The atten-
dance receptionist shook her head when she saw me.

"What is going on, Kerry?" she asked, her brow wrinkled.

I just shrugged.

In algebra, right after lunch, I couldn't keep my eyes open. I
rested my head on my open textbook, waking to drool on the page.
The teacher didn't notice or didn't care. I was invisible in this way

at school. But at Dorrian's it was different. Both Amy and I liked boys, but slowly it became clear that my want had a different flavor. The times we left Dorrian's having met no boys, Amy glanced at me on the drive home.

"What's the matter with you?"

"Nothing," I said.

"Is it because we aren't going home with some dudes?"

"Of course not," I said. I looked out the window so she couldn't see my face. My wanting was a cold shame.

"It's not that big of a deal," she said.

"I know. I didn't say it was." Below us, on the bridge, I could see the tiny, constant waves on the surface of the Hudson River.

"You care way too much," she said, her voice full of judgment.

The next time we went home with guys, I let one push his fingers inside me. "Can I fuck you?" he whispered, and although I said no, his whisper was like those waves rushing through me, building this thing inside me.

It was later that year that I lost my virginity to a kind boy I wasn't attracted to but whom I could trust. I didn't dare tell Amy. But from then on I slept with every boy who offered. I tried to fill myself with their bodies, with their desire for me, even though they disappeared as soon as they were done.

It wasn't that much later that other girls in my grade began to notice me. Popular girls, bad girls like me. We spent more and more time together, and I began to ignore Amy's calls. I was always busy. I always had plans. And over time she left me alone so I could be this new girl I had been becoming, different from her.

Jeanette

EVERYONE AT SCHOOL KNEW WHO SHE WAS. SHE HAD SEX with twin brothers who were two grades below her. This after working her way through her own grade's boys. She walked through the school hallways with long strides, head held high. She didn't care about the whispers or the blond girls' judgment. She didn't care that the junior girls called her gross and the junior boys called her easy. She was the opposite of me.

Her friends were the odd ones, the girls who would later become lawyers working for social justice or poetry professors or executive directors of nonprofits. They were girls boys didn't look at. They were thick thighed and broad shouldered, and I thought of them as strong. Once, I had dinner with them. I don't remember how this came to be, that I would join this group for one night, but I do remember feeling mute, unable to join the conversation, uncertain of my place with them. Jeanette told a story of a date she had with a guy in his early twenties whom she met at the gym. She mimicked the way he ate, shoveling his food into his mouth like a bulldozer. She told us he even ate the garnish while she'd looked on aghast. She laughed with us, her head bent back, mouth open. I could not imagine this, refusing a boy because of how he ate. I could hardly imagine refusing a boy at all.

Years later I heard more stories about what she had done in high school. Sex swings and cocaine snorted off a boy's penis and three guys at once. I had spent my entire adolescence full of shame for my desperation around boys, and Jeanette was right there the whole time, her head bent back, her mouth open, taking whatever she wanted.

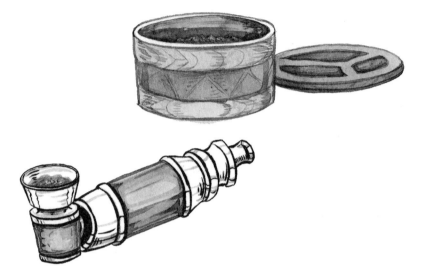

Heather

HEATHER TOLD ME THAT JASON HAD SEEN ME AT A PARTY and thought I was cute. Her boyfriend, Jeff, picked us up and got Jason, and that first night he said, "Sit on my lap," because there wasn't enough room in the car. He held onto me and rubbed my leg, and I was thrilled that I might have a normal boyfriend, not a one-night stand or a near miss or a guy who had another girlfriend and was just keeping me on the side.

We got high and then went for dinner at a Japanese restaurant. He was funny. I was funny. Heather and Jeff were funny. Everything felt right for the first time in forever. He went on vacation, and when he called he said he missed me, even though we hadn't had sex yet, but I loved that he said it, so I said it too. He came home with a woven bracelet for me and we had sex for the first time and everything was right.

Heather and Jeff had been together a long time. They fought in a way I'd never seen before, screaming and angry and jealous. Once, in the school parking lot, they hid on opposite sides of Jeff's car and chucked rolled up pieces of paper at one another, screaming, "I hate you!" "I hate you more!" With Jason, it wasn't like that. It was calm, but I wouldn't say it was easy. I felt what I always felt, what I walked around with on a daily basis, which was that I was not meant to be kept. I was not meant to be loved in the ways Heather was loved. No one would become enraged with jealousy about me. No one would care enough to throw things at me.

And, indeed, Jason began his slow retreat away from me just as I assumed he eventually would. And then it was Heather and me and sometimes Jeff. We still got high, and we still laughed so hard we peed. But always there remained this unsteady difference between us. She was lovable. I was not.

One day she left her wallet in a restaurant where we'd had lunch. She drove us back there, and she said, "You go get it. You're prettier than I am." And I understood for the first time ever that maybe I was wrong about me. Maybe she and I were the same.

Jennifer

THE FIRST TIME JENNIFER GAVE ME ATTENTION WAS when I offered her some of my father's cocaine. We cut it up on a cassette case in her Honda Accord. "Your shit. You go first," she said, handing me the case. I rolled up a dollar bill, something I learned from seeing rolled-up bills all over my father's apartment, and I sniffed a line. Instantly, my throat fluttered, and my brain lit up. She took the rolled bill and did the same.

"How come we haven't hung out before?" she asked.

On weekends I went to her father's house or she came to my apartment. She was best friends with other girls in our grade, but I hoped I could be one too.

We did a lot of cocaine.

We talked about our destroyed families.

Jennifer was beautiful, with long golden-brown legs and full lips. She had a grace I envied. Boys wanted her; although boys thought I was pretty, I didn't have her nonchalance. I was grabby, needy. I had not one bit of grace. She had stories from her past when she was a horseback rider. She had struggled briefly with an eating disorder. Those days were over now. We were seniors in high school, and then we graduated and went off to separate colleges.

The first winter break after freshman year of college, a small group of us gathered at Jennifer's father's house. Jennifer brought with her a friend from college, a coke dealer who wound up being one of my childhood friends. That friend brought one of his friends from high school, Will. Before I arrived, Will and Jennifer had been sleeping together. It was just here and there, when they felt like it. Often he went home instead.

One evening, Will slipped his hand into a hole in my jeans. For a moment I felt confused. Had he meant to do so? But I met his eyes and he smiled at me, his fingers caressing my skin, and my insides lit up in new ways.

I gave him a ride home that night. He acted perfectly normal, and I considered that I'd been imagining his touch, the look in his eyes. But when we arrived to his driveway, he kissed me, long and deep. He wormed his fingers into the hole in my jeans again and said, "You wore these just to make me crazy."

"I didn't," I said, breathless.

"Take me to your place."

I did. He slept over that night. And for the next few weeks we left Jennifer's house together, and he slept over each time.

One evening in the car, I asked, "What about Jennifer?"

"What about her?"

"Are you still sleeping with her too?"

"Nah," he said.

My throat tightened with joy. He chose me over Jennifer, the girl every boy wanted.

We went back to our colleges, and I reluctantly said goodbye to Will.

Summer came and all of us who had graduated the year before got in touch. There would be a reunion party. The night of the party I couldn't reach anyone. I left voicemails, but nobody called me back. When I arrived to the party Jennifer and her friends were already there.

"Don't you dare talk to us," one of them said.

My stomach dropped. "Why?"

"We know what you did," another one said. "With Will. You lied to Jennifer."

I looked at Jennifer, trying to meet her eyes, but she kept her head down.

"Jennifer," I said.

She didn't respond.

"I'm sorry," I said.

"Apology not accepted," the first girl said.

I left quickly, my eyes blurry with tears as I drove home. It was the last time I ever saw Jennifer.

A year after my memoir that told this story came out, Jennifer got in touch with me. We made a phone date and talked for two hours about all of it, about Will, about the issues I had with boys, about how I'd betrayed her and hated myself at the time. She cried, recounting those days. I did too. Amazing how all those years later you can feel just the same. All the old feelings come rushing in: *please like me, please don't hate me, please be my friend.* We promised we'd talk again and that the next time I came to New York we would try to get together. But of course we never did.

Sam

SAM MADE HERSELF VOMIT AFTER MEALS. SHE ENCOUR-
aged a few other women in the dorm to join her. They went together
to the bathroom while I waited in her room not wanting to hear the
sounds of gagging. I spent most of my time in her room. Sam, Meryl,
who lived in the room next to Sam's, and I were best friends, all
freshmen in college. It was a relief to have friends so quickly in this
new place where I had known no one. More than that, I adored Sam.
We met because she knew one of the Jennifers I'd been friends with
back in high school. There were three Jennifers, and she was my
least favorite. In fact, that Jennifer frightened me. She had a laugh
that brought out every one of my insecurities, a laugh that said, *I
see you for what you are.* But she was best friends with the other two
Jennifers, both whom I liked very much, so I was stuck with her.

Sam's dorm room was full of goodies: granola bars, choc-
olate, chips, soda. We spent much of our time talking about our
bodies. We were both thin, but we didn't see that, and we were
desperate to be thinner. We worked out constantly. We avoided the
cafeteria. As a result, I was always hungry, but Sam never seemed
hungry at all. In her room, I unwrapped granola and candy bars. I
ate them shamefully, embarrassed by my need, but I couldn't help
myself. I couldn't resist my constant neediness.

I remember she did this thing where she used her spit to
make bubbles on her tongue and then blew them into the air. She
did this over and over again. Little bubbles floating around her. I
was envious of that.

Her boyfriend went to a school in another state, and this was torture for her. The boys at school loved Sam. They all wanted to get with her. But she would have none of it, devoted as she was to her boyfriend. She spent hours on the phone with her boyfriend each night, her missing him a deep well of pain inside her. He loved her just as intensely, and so she couldn't understand my desperation around boys, how I didn't believe one could love me, how I gave myself always too willingly in the hopes of something more in return. I didn't know how to have what she had.

Over winter break I went home to New Jersey. Two of the Jennifers and I met up at one of their houses with two of that Jennifer's friends from college. Two guys, one with whom she'd been sleeping. The other one brought the cocaine. This was a Jennifer I loved and the Jennifer I feared. Five of us reconvened each night to snort lines and smoke cigarettes and laugh. Sometimes Jennifer disappeared into the bedroom with the boy. Then, one evening, that boy slipped his hand into the hole in my jeans near my crotch. Just like that. We were all laughing and snorting and smoking, and suddenly his hand was on me, and I could think of nothing else. He asked me to drive him home that night, and instead I wound up driving him back to my apartment, where I lived with my father.

I asked, "What about Jennifer?"

He said, "What about her?"

What I know now is that I didn't care about Jennifer. That's not accurate. I did care. I liked Jennifer a lot. I felt bad for what I'd done. But mostly I wanted this boy to pick me over her. I wanted to have something I never got: to be the one chosen.

This boy and I kept up our secret affair for the rest of winter break. Sometimes we left at the same time. Other times we left separately and met up later. He stopped sleeping with Jennifer and only slept with me, and I believed that Jennifer didn't care about it, which was a convenient belief for me to have.

Back at college, sitting in Sam's dorm room, I told her the whole thing. Even as I told her I knew it was a bad idea. She and the other Jennifer who was there each night I snuck around behind their backs were closer than I was with Sam. But I couldn't help myself. I wanted to prove myself. I wanted to show her someone could choose me too. I wanted.

One afternoon, we went running—Sam, Meryl, and me. We returned to her room, sweating and exhausted, and Meryl went to take a shower.

Sam's pile of granola bars sat on her desk. I reached for one. "Is it okay to take one?" I asked.

"Never stopped you before."

I pulled my hand back.

"Don't you ever eat in your own room?" she asked.

"Yeah," I started. "I just like to be here. With you."

She turned away from me to gather her towel and toiletries. Her back was narrow and stiff, like a shut door.

Later, she called. "Are you coming back, or what?"

But something had spun into motion and there would be no going back.

She told Jennifer during spring break, while I used those two weeks to try to see that boy I'd risked all my friendships for. He was apathetic. I could come see him or not. No sweat off his back. No skin off his shoulder.

By the time we returned to school Sam had stopped calling me. She and Meryl stayed tight, and I floated again into friendlessness. But I found a boyfriend, someone to love me. I spent every last second with him. By summer break all the Jennifers knew about what I had done. They confronted me at the first party of the summer, where all of us who'd graduated the year before were having a reunion. It was the mean Jennifer who spoke to me, who told me I was never to come near the three of them again.

At home I cried and smoked cigarettes and waited for my boyfriend to arrive. He drove down from Maine so I wouldn't have to be alone, even though I was leaving the next day for a cruise to celebrate my grandfather's eightieth birthday. I arrived to that boat sleepless and disoriented. I had no idea how to begin again. I do remember spending much of that trip standing on the deck, watching the way the boat pushed aside the bubbling water as it forged ahead.

Kelly

KELLY WASN'T AN ATTRACTIVE GIRL. SHE HAD FRIZZY black hair and a stout body. She introduced me to Joni Mitchell's *Blue* album. We listened to it daily, lying head to feet on her bed in the dorm, and we spoke of our own heartaches, the rivers and planes and cases of you. I don't remember losing her. But years later I heard she killed herself, which was both a surprise and not a surprise.

Sharon

PRETTY. IS THERE A MORE HORRIBLE WORD? A MORE
insipid one? A more perfect one? When I was ten I watched my mother
put on makeup. I sat on the closed toilet seat wanting to learn what
it meant to be a woman, to be pretty. Once, I asked my mother if I
was pretty. She hesitated, and then she said I was cute. My sister
was the pretty one. She says now she never said such a thing, but
this is how I remember it. Leif, my boyfriend in college, said, "You
could be a model." That's ridiculous, of course. He was hopped up
on sex hormones, on love. I could be no such thing.

In college Sharon was pretty. No, she was beautiful. She was
what all us women who were her friends wanted to be. I'll describe
her, her outsides. She had long, brown hair. Brown eyes. Perfectly
placed eyes and nose and mouth. Her skin was chestnut brown.
Inside, she was also beautiful, but that is less relevant to this story.

When Leif and I first got together, I was in a state of euphoria.
He was beautiful. I had lusted for him from afar, and then finally, one
night at a party on the third floor of my building, I convinced him
to come back to my apartment, just him and me. I lured him with
weed. I knew it was his weakness. And I didn't believe I was interesting enough to attract him without it. That night we wound up in bed
together. We stayed there for twenty-four hours, leaving only to pee.
Around nine the next night, we determined we probably needed
food. We showered together, and then we went to a Thai restaurant.
We sat across from each other, shy, feeling strange with our utensils,
with civilized behavior after our animal, sensual body connection.

I didn't see him again for a week. He had been seeing another woman. I didn't know that at this point. I only know I craved him like a drug. While cleaning one evening, I found a folded piece of paper under my bed. It was covered with musical notations, short statements. It was his. I covered my smile with my hand. Later that night I called him to say he left something at my place. It looked important. Of course it didn't really, but it worked. He came over and we stayed in bed another twenty-four hours.

He broke up with the other woman, and for the next few weeks I walked around campus high on him, on his smell, on his touch. In each other's presence we could barely hold ourselves back. Once, his friend leaned over, sitting next to him in class. He said, "You smell like girl."

Over the next few months, Leif practically lived in my apartment. His own apartment was in the same building as the woman he'd dumped for me. He didn't want to have to deal with that, he told me. I woke in the morning, leaving him in my bed, and went to class. By the time I returned he was gone at his afternoon music classes. He stayed in the studio until late at night—two or three in the morning. I'd be asleep, restless, waiting, aware of every rustle outside, every footstep, until finally I heard him unlatch the door and come to me.

When summer came I begged him to stay with me on campus, but he had to go home to be with his band. I visited him often, staying in his parents' house, literally hiding upstairs until they left for work each day because I was embarrassed by my presence in their home, embarrassed by my desperation for their son. When classes started up again I was relieved. I wouldn't have to find ways to be near him, to have him in my grasp. He'd be right there on campus. But I was wrong. However much time he had for me, however much he thought of me, it was never enough. So, I pushed for him to move in with me. I planned it perfectly. First, I'd move to the same building where one of his best friends lived, the same one who said he smelled like girl all those months ago, and then I'd be overwhelmed with the cost. I'd say, "You're always here any-

way." I'd say, "You can have your own room so you still have your own space. I'd say, "I won't bother you, I promise." I'd say, "Please."

But he said no, not yet. It was too soon, too big of a commitment. So he moved into an apartment with Sharon. The beautiful one. Granted, her boyfriend also lived with them. She and her boyfriend shared one room and Leif was in the other, but I was too aware of the ways in which I could be forgotten. He would see her emerge from the bathroom in a towel. He would have opportunities to connect with her, just sitting at the table. He would see her beauty and I would disappear.

When all of us hung out, or when I went to their apartment, things were different between Sharon and me. Where once we laughed and connected, now we felt shy and uncertain. Or I did. I felt shy and uncertain. I felt insecure. And ugly. I felt ugly around her.

He told me about one incident in which he made spaghetti for all three of them. She said he needed to put olive oil in the boiling water, and he said, "Kerry doesn't do that," and they had a moment during which they looked at each other, uncomfortable, knowing there was an unexpected competition they hadn't expected. He told me this with a laugh, but it meant to me that he did think of her as my competition. I knew I could never really compete with Sharon.

Eventually Sharon and her boyfriend broke up. Leif told me later they had a horrible fight. He called her a cheating slut and threw things across the room while Sharon cried. She hadn't done anything, Leif said. She hadn't cheated. It bothered me that he felt the need to defend her. But because they broke up they had to give up their apartment, so he finally, begrudgingly moved in with me. Sharon and I stayed in each other's circle. She was so nice. She was really like one of the nicest people you'll ever meet. She worked hard in school, studying psychology. She wanted to do something important in the world. Men continued to lust after her, and again and again she wound up with ones who treated her with disdain. For her beauty. I knew this. I understood the cruel irony of it, how unfair it was for Sharon, who was just a good person trying to do good things. She would always be punished for her beauty. I punished her too. I kept her at arm's length because being around her highlighted the ways in which I wasn't anywhere near as beautiful, and it made me feel bad about myself. She needed friends. She needed people to love her for who she was when so many wouldn't. I still regret that.

Storey

EVEN HER NAME WAS ROMANTIC. STOREY. IF I EVER GIVE birth to a girl, I thought, I'll name her Storey, but I never did. She was beautiful and sexy with dark hair and long legs, eyes like a cat's. She slunk around my best friend's apartment when she came to hang out, smoked cigarettes, drank beer from bottles. Wouldn't look at me. Now I realize it was likely because she didn't know me, didn't trust me. At our college the rumors about her were endless. Cocaine. Whiskey. But at the time I believed it was because I wasn't interesting enough for her, wasn't cool enough. Wasn't fill-in-the-blank enough. Her boyfriend's name was Jim Morrison. Really. He looked just like the singer, too. Lanky and sexy with long hair and an ego as big as his name. The rumors were that they fought often. They fought loud and hard, and they used their fists.

Later that year, when I'd landed Leif, I'd think maybe we could be the new Storey and Jim, full of passion and wildness. But he never loved me as much as I loved him. He always kept me at arm's length while I pushed and pushed for more. Leif would never have screamed at me about being a slut. I would never throw something at him and stomp out the door. I didn't walk away from men. Not ever. I held them in my clutches as tightly as I could until they broke free.

Recently I looked her up on Facebook, and I was surprised to see she's married with two kids. She's just a woman, a normal, pretty woman living her life. She surely always was.

Anu

I SAID, "I HATE THAT MY THIGHS TOUCH."
She said, "My thighs have never touched," and walked away
gracefully, unaware of the harm she'd done.

Melissa

WE MET AT A WRITERS CONFERENCE. OUR CONNECTION was instant and whole. But one time, we were in a coffee shop, and she said she didn't feel good. She put her head between her legs. "I'm so dizzy," she said. In the next moment she slid to the floor, onto her stomach. I remember the slow-motion movement, the graceful stretch of it, and then how she began to twitch, her body something alien and unknown, out of control. Mostly I remember the wetness that bloomed at her crotch and down her legs. I yelled for help, and somebody called 911. She awoke confused and exhausted, and I wouldn't let her get up until the EMTs arrived. The barista brought her water and apple juice. This had never happened to her before, she told the medic. He took her blood pressure and pulse. He gave her the option of going to the hospital, but she decided against it. Eventually he helped her stand up, and I walked her back to her apartment.

She called, but I made excuses for why I couldn't see her again. I didn't tell her the truth, which was that I was frightened by her, by the looseness of her body, by a body beyond a body. I didn't like the idea of such entropy. I was scared, really, of her body, and although I felt terrible shame about it, I couldn't bring myself to see her again.

Zainab

ON OUR FIRST ORIENTATION DAY OF THE MFA PROGRAM there was nothing about her that would suggest we would be good friends. She seemed suburban to me, married for the second time at twenty-six, wearing lipstick, foundation, and straightened hair that, in my opinion, all worked to hide her natural beauty. She was short and skinny, and on that first day I noticed a nervous laugh that I'd learn to stop noticing later. I like to think back to this day and my first impressions of Zainab. She grew too powerful eventually, like a monster. But on this day she was just a young nervous girl who wanted to write, like I was.

She pursued me. I'm almost sure of that, but memory is a tricky thing. And Zainab wasn't the kind of person who pursued anything. Everyone pursued her. But this is how I remember it. I had been closest with Stacey, another woman in our program. Zainab slid her way into our friendship. She had been watching us. She must have been. Because she knew exactly how to meet our overly expressive sexuality, our flirtations with faculty, disruptive behavior in the composition-teaching courses we had to take. There is a photo that I've since lost in a move of the three of us, all in short, tight black dresses, our brown hair, hips out, arms up as we danced. In the background is a male faculty member watching us. We were always trying to get watched. She convinced me that Stacey was out of control, and gradually she made me all hers.

Zainab was the program's star. I didn't know this until I neared graduation. The program director had flown her into the university town and taken her out for dinner. I was just beginning to understand that the world treated Zainab exactly as she demanded to be treated, like a sort of royalty. Zainab grew up in the caste system in India. She had servants. She actually called them that: servants. And she, the oldest and only girl, had been treated like a queen.

She brought one chapter from the novel she claimed she was writing into our workshop. The first chapter. She brought it in again and again, changing it each time. Other times, she passed on bringing her work in. She was sick and couldn't make it on her workshop days. Or she was going to have to be out of town. Her novel was a thinly veiled fiction of her experience of being physically abused while in an arranged marriage. Over cigarettes and wine she described to me how her current husband had saved her from that marriage. That's how she said it. He *rescued* her, as though she had been drowning, as though an enemy had hauled her over his shoulder and run off, and this man had come to retrieve her, like a prince from a fairy tale.

A poet in our program, Tim, pursued her. A top literary agent pursued her even though she had no finished book. These are the sorts of things that happened to her. Meanwhile I forced crinkled paper with my phone number into men's hands. I left notes to get them to think of me. I got rejections from literary magazines. Zainab had this philosophy that there was enough of everything for everybody. Just because she had something didn't mean I couldn't. She only put herself out there when she knew with razor sharp clarity that only good would come back. She didn't *allow* rejection.

Eventually Tim rescued her from her marriage, and they moved together to San Francisco. I moved back to Portland with a man who didn't love me, who couldn't love me because he was too in love with his drugs, and I worked as adjunct faculty in composition at community colleges. I wrote when I could. Tim applied for jobs teaching composition, and Zainab worked on her book. More agents pursued her, and she was offered a seven-figure, two-book deal from FSG. She had not even finished one of them.

I visited her twice. The first time was to be her maid of honor. The second time was just before she and Tim got pregnant. She showed me the office where she wrote every day. She showed me the vase she thought I got her for their wedding. When I didn't recognize it, she laughed. I didn't clarify what I really got them, which was all I could afford. I bought them wind chimes, and I attached a note about how every time they heard it ring they would be reminded of their love. Those chimes were nowhere to be seen, and I felt ashamed. I constantly felt like I was scrambling to be good enough in relation to Zainab and constantly missing the mark. I could never have anything I wanted, but she got everything. What's more, she expected it. I wish so much I could go back to being that younger Kerry and tell Zainab that she was no better than I was, that I was whole and good and just right.

Zainab almost died while delivering her son. Everything in her life was like this, drama filled and story worthy. She almost *died*. Really? I asked. *Why would I lie about that?* And then the baby was here, and she didn't die. But she started to have problems with Tim. She sent me long, melodramatic letters in which she described how Tim was harmful and terrible and just all-around bad. She sent me emails saying the same thing. One began: "This cannot continue. I cannot go on like this. I whisper my son's name at night, and pray he will be safe inside his name."

I wrote her back suggesting that maybe she was caught in a pattern in which men rescued her from other men and she remained a victim. She was furious. She could not *believe* I would talk to her like this. Didn't I support her? Didn't I want her to be happy? Did I think she was a *liar*? So many women talked to me like this. I didn't know it then but Zainab was in a long line that had begun with my mother. So I apologized. I had been trained well by my mother and by a handful of other women who I was not to ever suggest weren't perfect. I was not to ever have a voice in the face of their needs. She wrote back after the apology, praising me for being such a good friend.

The next day, I mailed her a letter. It read:

Dear Zainab,

We are very different people, and I don't believe we want the same things from our friendship. So, I'm ending it now. I wish you all the best.
    Love,
    Kerry.

I never heard from her again.

Three years later, I saw her image in *Vogue*. She was as beautiful as always. Her novel had come out, the one she'd been working on since graduate school. I wanted badly to call to congratulate her, but I didn't. Instead, I started writing. That was when I started writing again, with the ghost of Zainab as my muse.

Alison

ALISON AND I MET FRESH FROM GRADUATE SCHOOL. It was impossible to get full-time jobs in our field without books or much experience yet, so we both applied and got jobs at a college preparatory organization looking for people to teach high school students how to write college acceptance letters. We met at the all-day training we had to attend, which was held in a hotel conference center. I knew I wanted her as my friend when she leaned toward me and said, "If that woman uses the phrase 'writing process' one more time I'm going to stab her with my No. 2 pencil."

We spent lots of our friendship in bars meeting boys. I was flirty, smiling, and eager, while Allison wore an expression of doom. More often than not I was the one who attracted the guys to our table.

I told her, "You have to smile!"

She said, "Why would I smile when it's all going to end in smoke and ashes?"

I laughed, but I also understood what she meant. I felt desperate about boys. I needed them to want me in order to feel that I was worthwhile, and boys, well, you know how much boys love needy girls. I shared this with Allison and she shook her head.

"You don't have to worry about that," she said. "You're young and pretty. I'm the one who has to worry."

Alison was a good seven years older than me, so while I wanted to get married as some proof of my worth in the world, her desire to get married was more like panic. There was the old maid thing that still hung around our culture after all these centuries. There was also the baby thing. She talked about it often, and when I suggested she had plenty of time, that she was pretty too, she said, "That's easy for you to say."

Eventually Alison and I both landed boyfriends. Mine was one of those experiments all late-twenty-something women try: a great guy I wasn't actually attracted to. It lasted about six months before I finally gave up. Alison's was exactly her type, but he was in his early twenties and, although in love with her, wasn't interested in settling down and becoming a family man. She secretly hoped he would change his mind over time. Meanwhile both of our writing and teaching careers grew. She got herself a full-time teaching gig, and I signed with an agent. Soon after, I met the guy I would marry.

I think it was when I got engaged that things began to slide, though I didn't see it at all at the time. She still met me for drinks. We still took walks through the neighborhood and spoke often on the phone. I spoke animatedly about my wedding plans while she swirled the beer in her glass.

Then someone at the college where she worked introduced her to a man. She liked him, she said. He was basically good, and he was her age. She had some worries. He had an angry streak, and he had already turned that anger on her. He also drank a lot. But he wanted a baby too, so she got pregnant. We shared information about my wedding shower and her baby shower, and when we mistakenly planned them for the same date she said, "Yours is just a wedding shower, Kerry. Mine is for a real live person."

As my wedding neared, she sent her regrets. Her baby was due right at the same time. I understood, of course, although all these years later I still wonder about the coincidence. The day she came home from the hospital with her baby boy I went right over to see him. He was so tiny and fragile, his little head bobbing at her chest. I was happy for her.

A year later I got pregnant, and soon after my baby came I sold my first book. It wasn't long after this time that I called Alison

just to say hi or check in or tell her something and she never called back. I tried again, and again her cell went to voicemail. As the days passed, my paranoia about her not returning my calls turned into reality. She actually wasn't going to call me back. I combed every moment we'd spent together over the past couple months. I tried to remember everything I'd said. Had she misinterpreted something I said? Had I hurt her unintentionally?

As the weeks passed my mind went to a more painful place: what was it about me that made her leave?

I didn't see her for two years, and then one day I went to Wild Oats to pick up some food for my son. I was eight months pregnant with my second baby by then, and I was in my overworn maternity pants. My face had broken out, and my ankles were swollen. As I rounded an aisle, there she was, talking happily and intimately with a friend. My heart jumped into my throat. I stopped breathing. I backed up my cart, walked quickly away from it, and went out the sliding doors to the parking lot. As I got into my car I saw her familiar Subaru, the dream catcher hanging from the rearview mirror, the crack along the bottom of the windshield. How had I missed it as I came inside? It was as familiar as an old lover's.

I barely made it home before the tears came.

"What is wrong with me?" I asked my husband. "Why did she do that?"

He held me. He told me I did nothing.

But I didn't believe him. All my life I'd assumed—as so many of us do—that there was something unlovable about me. It's why I'd had those issues with boys. Allison knew that. All my life I'd held that shameful belief, then I had trusted her with it and, in my mind, she had confirmed it as true.

It was another two years before I saw her again. We were in front of the same Whole Foods. I had my younger son with me in the cart. She was alone. She greeted me as though we were friendly acquaintances, and we caught up. I told her about my older son's diagnosis with autism, the strains on my marriage, a couple bad reviews for my second book. She cocked her head and nodded, told me she was sorry, and then she told me everything in her life was just great.

I said, "I'd really like to know what happened with us."

She smiled and nodded again but said nothing. And I left feeling as though a hole had been borne through my insides. Why did I keep opening myself up like this? Why couldn't I just keep my mouth shut?

The next time I saw her my husband and I had separated and I was with my boyfriend. She said, "Who's this?" And I stupidly told her about my separation. She cocked her head and apologized again, and I left furious with myself.

The last time I saw her I was prepared. She walked into a literary event where I knew many people and she knew only the woman with whom she arrived. She saw me and started to smile, and this time I met her eyes but looked away. I ignored her the entire night, and I stayed busy chatting with people who hadn't done something that led to wasting so much time wondering if I was unlovable.

Stacey

I MISS ALL OF MY EX-FRIENDS. THEY ARE STAMPED ONTO my heart like old romances, lost loves. They are part of me in ways no one warned me they would be. Had I known, I would have chosen more carefully. I would have better thought through what we did to one another, how we used each other, and how we split apart. I will always miss Stacey. The fun we had together was incomparable. She was hilarious, witty, sharp, and loving. She believed she was bound for greatness. Once she told me she just knew she would be famous someday. She was a poet, a good one, but not a great one. She never did become famous, and I wonder how she's doing with that truth.

Here's what I think happened between us: Stacey needed a friend who would teach her about self-growth. I needed a friend to mentor. It's a terrible setup for friendship. I will never do that again. But at the time it felt good. She would do anything for me, and over time she learned I would only do so much for her. That's one way to look at what happened. She began to change, to come into her own, and that person was not someone I could connect with anymore. That's another way.

Stacey was a great storyteller. I could never tell whether she truly believed her stories, or if she wanted to so badly that she did. For a period of time, right before our friendship came to an end, she dated a guy named Mario. Mario Gotti. As in the Gotti family from New York. What a Gotti was doing in Portland, I don't know. Stacey argued that this is where his family kept him so he wouldn't be found out. He called her regularly, trying to woo her. In a reasonable manner, she didn't buy that he was actually from the Gotti mob family. But then one time he put her on a conference call with Joe Pesci.

"You don't really believe that was Joe Pesci," I said when she told me later.

"It sure sounded like him," she asserted.

Later, I told a mutual friend Terri about it. "I'm sure there are lots of people who do great Joe Pesci impressions," she said.

That's when it occurred to me. "Wait, just because Joe Pesci has been in mob movies, that doesn't mean he knows the Gotti family!"

We laughed.

"Oh, Stacey," Terri said. At that point we both found her endearing.

Next, Mario gave her gifts. Ugly gold jewelry and sports equipment. Every time he visited her he brought more.

"The jewelry is from Fred Meyer?" I asked when she brought it out to show me. There were gold bracelets with emerald stones, diamond earrings, and necklaces studded with both.

"So?"

"He's a Gotti," I said. "He can't shop at Tiffany's?"

She shrugged and shoved the jewelry back into their boxes.

And then came the brain tumor. She told Terri and me together, sitting in my backyard with wine. He needed help, she told us, and she was going to help him. She went to his apartment every day. Once she called crying because he'd been bleeding from his eyes.

"Do brain tumors cause eye bleeding?" I asked.

She was getting tired of my questions.

Stacey and I spent less and less time together. I missed my friend, the person I'd respected. The knowledge that our friendship couldn't last wove through my veins, as much as I tried to ignore it.

A few weeks later she invited me out for a drink. She came to pick me up. We parked near the bar and she turned off the engine. She took a big breath and turned to me.

"I have to tell you something," she said. "You have to promise not to tell anyone."

"Of course."

Her expression was serious. "The aliens are coming."

"I'm sorry?"

"Mario knows because the government leaked it to the Gotti family. No one else is privy. But listen, everyone in his family, including girlfriends, are allowed to bring ten people on the spaceship to safety, and I want you to know that you and Michael, who was my fiancé at the time, are two of my ten."

I held my face as still as possible. "Thanks, Stace."

My stomach felt like a leaden rock. Clearly our friendship had come to an end. We had our drink, and later I called Terri to tell her.

"Oh my god, she's completely lost her mind," Terri said.

"What do we do?"

"There's nothing we can do. She's on her own journey. She'll figure it out eventually."

And she did. But she wasn't fully convinced until she took all the Fred Meyer jewelry back to the store and learned that it was all fake.

Sue Jin

EZRA CAME INTO THE WORLD SLOWLY, HIS TINY BODY disinterested outside its comforts in the womb. But all children must begin somewhere, and he began that morning on July 25, 2003. I pushed for hours, my own body exhausted and wrecked from this marathon. But we worked together, and eventually he arrived, blond haired and red skinned. My baby boy. My first perfect thing. I knew him entirely: the freckle by his belly button, the little line on his nose, like a lion's. So when he grew into a toddler who wasn't speaking while all the other toddlers his age were I grew frightened.

I was part of a moms group that convened once a week to combat the boredom of new motherhood. We sat with our babies on our laps, chatting. Then we followed them as they crawled and toddled, and now all the children were using words. They asked for snacks, for toys, for mommy to pick them up. Ezra stayed silent. He played on his own or he sat on my lap observing the other kids.

Inside a panic was brewing. There was something different, something wrong. There was something not right about my perfect baby boy. I grew more silent in the group. I skipped it a lot, claiming exhaustion.

One time I said carefully, "I'm worried about Ezra's development."

Sue Jin heard me. Her son Timon spoke fluently, was advanced for his age. Sometimes hearing him speak hurt in a way I couldn't admit.

"We take Timon camping a lot. I believe that's why he's developed so fast. Nature helps kids' development."

We never went camping with Ezra. We couldn't. He woke throughout the night, and he would likely wander away while we slept. Was I failing him in this way? This part of me, this part that would grow with shame and fear and grief over the next few years as I came to terms with Ezra's autism, heard what she surely hadn't intended: it's your fault he isn't developing typically.

Theresa

I MADE HER COME OVER TO OBSERVE Ezra. She worked with children in mental health. I needed her to tell me something. I needed things from her she could never give me. I made her come over again and again. I said, "Tell me," again and again. Then a friend who is no longer a friend said, "She told me she's tired of hearing you talk about Ezra, that that is all you do."

So I stopped making her come over. I stopped making her tell me things. I allowed the grief to wash over me, which is exactly what I needed to do anyway. I don't blame Theresa for this. I wanted to get away from me too.

Terri

I WAS NEW TO PORTLAND THAT SPRING AND HAD NEVER seen such flowers: pink petals floating down from cherry trees, a snowstorm of them on the streets; blue hydrangeas and dinner-plate dahlias; flowers with beards and spikes; magnolias and spherical alliums. A whole world I didn't know. This was when I first met Terri. She had lived there all her life. She had seen these sights every spring, but I was wide-eyed with wonder, with a sense of possibility, with displacement. A health food grocery store had just opened on Division, a short bike ride from the house share I lived in with three hippies and two dogs. I needed a job, so I went there, resume in a crisp manila folder. Terri was assistant manager at the juice bar. When she interviewed me she pushed my resume back.

"I don't need that," she said. "Just tell me about who you are."

I didn't know who I was. I was twenty-three. I'd just had a heart-bending breakup with my first real love. I was in Portland because I ran there to be with a good friend after my relationship imploded. I thought maybe I was a writer.

We stayed in touch when I went away for my MFA in creative writing. She had a high school degree. She had so many ideas of what she could be if she went back to school. I shared her enthusiasm, believed she'd make a great counselor, teacher, music thera-pist ... but she never did any of it.

When I returned, another relationship ended, this time with a drug dealer. What was I doing? I didn't know. I moved across the street from Terri and we spent every day together, talking and talking and dissecting my life. I chose men who were so wrong for me, and then I desperately needed them to choose me, but they never did.

"What do *you* want," she asked me.

I didn't know yet.

We went out for coffee or glasses of wine and people said, "Are you sisters?" We laughed and told them we were best friends. But it was true. We had begun to look alike, like mirrors of the other. We got mistaken for each other often. Our love ran deep. We talked all day, and then we got home and called each other on the phone. It was like new romance, when you can't get enough.

One night we went to a bar and I saw a boy. Dark, shaggy hair, sultry eyes. Just my type. He and I met eyes, and Terri saw the flicker in my expression.

I smiled at the man when I stood and went to the back of the bar where the ladies' room was. My heart was in my throat, the blood rushing beneath my skin. The man's attention was like a sharp drug in my veins. I peed and then checked myself in the mirror. My cheeks were flushed from the wine, my hair full. I looked good.

When it was time to go, Terri and I stood and the man watched. He made a face that suggested he was bummed I was leaving. He waved goodbye, and I waved back. Men always needed me less than I needed them.

"Did you see that?" I said to Terri as we walked to her car. "That guy waved goodbye to me."

"He was looking at me too, you know," she said. "When you were in the bathroom, he smiled at me too."

I didn't say anything. I wasn't sure what I could say. My stomach felt heavy and thick. My throat tight. I was intensely aware of a pimple on my chin that I'd concealed carefully before going out. Surely everyone could see it. I waited for her to unlock the car door, and then I sat quietly next to her. I opened the window and closed my eyes, hoping the cool night air would wash away my frustration.

The next day, though, it was still bothering me. When she called I took a breath.

"That was weird when you said that guy was looking at you too."

"Well, Kerry. He was."

"Even so, I guess I don't know why you needed to tell me that."

She sighed. "You know, I grew up with sisters who overshadowed me. They were always getting the attention. And you just need so much with men. That's why I did it."

I should have taken this conversation as a warning. A person who wasn't me—who wasn't so desperate for connection, no matter how it came—would have. A different sort of person might have thought that Terri was dangerous. Terri was fun, and she was good to me. But she also always needed to be right, always needed to be one step above me. She would never admit that in my tendency to choose people who would harm me she was one of them.

After years of mistakes with men, I met Michael, the man I would marry. Terri stayed up with me all night before the wedding, my excitement too great, and then she sang at the ceremony.

I believed in our friendship. There was so much that was good about it. But life brings with it challenges you can't always foresee. For me, life brought Ezra, my autistic son. Not that he was a challenge, not that he was difficult, but the grief and fear that came with who he wound up being sent me reeling. I couldn't believe that I had ever thought anything in my life was hard before.

Terri thought I was being neurotic. She didn't believe in autism. She thought I needed to relax, to not care about what others thought, to stop worrying all the time. She tried to relate her own experience to mine, but there was no way to do so. This was mine and mine alone. Michael went into his own private grief, and I began an emotional affair.

When Michael and I separated, I slept with men. I did so swiftly and without regard for anything but my emptiness. Michael and I, still living together, spoke about what was happening. We were loving and kind. We meant no harm to each other. This wasn't about mistakes anymore. This wasn't about bad choices.

One night we tried to rekindle the marriage, and because I told Terri everything I told her we had sex. Two days later Terri yelled at me, livid, disgusted. She said, "You always made bad choices." I didn't understand what she meant, why she would do this to me. Was she mad that I had sex with my husband? I understood two years later, long after our friendship blew up, after I had moved on from Michael and was in a new relationship. Michael's sister confessed that Terri had called her soon after that day she yelled at me. Terri and his sister hardly knew one another, and she didn't know why she was calling until Terri told her I had a sexually transmitted disease. She told her I had given it to Michael. I had no STD, and I'd done nothing of the sort. Sometimes friendships reach their natural end. Terri and I were done with one another, had grown apart. I think that's why Terri made up these stories. People do crazy things amid breakups. They build fantasies. They lash out and try to hurt people they used to love. They do what they need to do to make sense of love's ending.

Still, Terri is the only friend I don't miss.

Unnamed

I HEARD SHE GOT TOGETHER FOR DRINKS WITH ANOTHER woman and trash-talked my family. I heard she worked to get my husband fired. I heard she told another friend a whole bunch of lies about things I said, and that friend still feels she can't trust me. I heard she contacted one of my editors and tried to ruin me. I heard she still says she misses me. I heard that after our friendship combusted she told someone, "She's the one writing a whole book about difficult friendships, not me."

Lesley

WE MET THROUGH MUTUAL FRIENDS AND IMMEDIATELY liked each other. We make each other laugh in ways I haven't since I was much younger, before divorce, before autism, before loss. She lost her best friend of thirty-five years just before we met, and she missed her intensely, hated her with the same intensity, and loved her too. I understood. She was smart and thoughtful and deeply compassionate. Sometimes with my friends I feel like I did when I was ten, desperately in love, terrified of losing this one, worried she doesn't love me as much as I love her. We need this, don't we? To define our relationships. You're my best friend. My only. I'm always careful to say one of my best friends because I don't want to disappoint or to invest too much in just one person. Because I want us to be okay. My friendships can feel at times like an addiction, like I can't live without at least one friend who I can turn to whenever I need, who will never leave me, who is mine, who is the most. That other one was my best friend and it didn't work out. But this one, this one is my true best friend. This one is for good.

My husband says, "I wish you'd be more careful."

I reply, "I can't."

Jennifer

IN HIGH SCHOOL EVERYONE WAS NAMED JENNIFER. TWO were good friends, and about four others were semi-friends. One was a frenemy. I once had a friend who gave me a poem she wrote called "The Jennies." It was about two girls who every other girl wants to be. I ruined my friendships with the two Jennifers who I was close with. I lost touch with the other Jennifers I hardly knew. Sometimes I feel haunted by the mean Jennifer, whose cruel laugh used to cut into everything I feared was true about me.

Decades after high school, though, one of the Jennifers came back. Not one of the ones I was friends with or even semi-friends with. This is another Jennifer. You never know what will happen in the future, who will come back, and who will go away. Jennifer and I are close. She is one of my favorite people. We have both been through the things you go through as you age: divorces, children, addiction, loss. I have figured out that the formula is kindness. Don't be an asshole. Don't try to hurt people. Try hard to have boundaries and limit expectations and take responsibility for your own heart. Because you never know who will return in all their truth and beauty.